GOOD TO GO!!!

WHAT EVERY MAN LIVES TO HEAR.

Robert L. Mann Jr.

DEDICATIONS

This book is dedicated to the many men that fought in wars and laid down their lives for our freedom. Army, Navy, Air Force, and Marines...

A special dedication goes out to my children, Donovan Lee, Robert Devon, and Carter Simone. Daddy is doing this for you all. Never give up on your dreams and always know Daddy's got you... Love you all.

CONTENTS

ACKNOWLEDGEMENTS

ow can I not begin without giving my Heavenly Father all praise? I take this time to thank you Daddy for allowing me, your son, to experience various issues in my life. When I was being selfish, thinking You were only teaching me through all I have gone through, here, you show me that these issues were given to me so that I can have a testimony to share with my brothers and sisters in need. All praises and thanks are for You first. Thank you, Daddy.

Next, thank you to my family - the Mann Klan - my parents, Pastor Robert and Juanita and my older brothers, Calvin and Michael. Thank you for encouraging and praying for me. When I was going through things over and over again, thank you for taking the time to tell me that things wouldn't always be this way and for reminding me of the promises that God has for me. Keep praying. I need them. To my rib, my heart, and the one God kept for me - Kimberly Mann (CHAP) - baby, thank you for standing by my side through thick and thin; good and bad. Thank you for the opportunity to love you for a couple of forevers.

To my team who has worked hard with me in getting this book ready for the world, I say thank you. From your feedback in what I should change to "Don't change anything at all. I thank you. To my pastors and friends, James Doggett, Sr., Damian Chandler, Delbleaire Snell, Alfonzo Greene III, and Kyle Crawford, thank you all for allowing me the opportunity to express my passion and just for being there overall so I could talk and for keeping me on the right paths. I thank you. My editor and Fantasy Football partner, Jennifer Patterson. Jen, thank you for your time spent assisting me in preparing my story.

To the men and women I have had the pleasure of serving alongside both in the military and in service for God, thank you. To Parris Island 3rd Battalion. Kilo Co.; Okinawa Japan Camp Foster 3rd Transportation Support Battalion; Schwab House; Division Won; 29 Palms California H&S Battalion; To all my Dogs of the United States Marine Corps - Charge On, Leathernecks... Hooorahhh!!!

To the men of Frontline Ministry, thank you all for the prayers, laughs, pains, arguments, and fellowship. Men need to hear and see you all. Don't stop recruiting men and fighting for the Army of God.

To the men who I have spent several days with just talking and getting to hang out with when times were rough - Gary Moore, Marius Hill, Roland Scott, Chandler Lucas (Big Luke), and Shannon Austin, my accountability partner - bro, thank you for the countless talks and the motivation you have given me. God has a work for you and we are going to keep on moving. No matter what... I AM WE. Thank you, big brother.

Thank you all,

Robert L. Mann

INTRODUCTION

"Sit down; let me explain what the Marine Corps have to offer."

As the Recruiter sat me down, he pulled out tabs with names of various jobs on them. If you have ever been to a recruiter's office or had a recruiter come to your house, you will remember these tabs. "All Marines will be trained in combat and will all become lean mean fighting machines, but these jobs are what will become your career and what you will be able to transfer from the military into the civilian world." I scrolled through several of the tabs and came up with three that I thought I would like - Supply, Communications, and Intelligence (Intel for short). As the meeting continued, we talked about what next steps, everything I would be doing in boot camp, and what the Marine Corps could do for me. It got me all pumped up to sign my name right then and there. When I tell you that my recruiter knew what he was doing - the boy was bad. Some people will tell you how their recruiter told them lies just to get them to sign up. No. Not mine. Staff Sergeant Harrison told me the good and the bad. How I would love it and hate it at the same time. He got me so hyped about signing that before I knew it, I had a pen in my hand signing everything. I took the practice Armed Services Vocational

Aptitude Battery (ASVAB), signed for my background check, and awaited my trip to Nashville, Tennessee to the Military Entrance Processing Station (MEPS) where I would raise my hand and swear to become one of The Few, The Proud, to become a Marine.

With all of this behind me, I began running every day, working out, and getting ready for something. I still didn't know what to expect, but I was going to be ready for it. Everything checked out. I received orders to report to the Marine Corps Recruit Depot at Parris Island, South Carolina on January 24, 1999. It was official. I was on my way. During Christmas of 1998, I went to Houston, Texas to spend time with my entire family - Mom, Dad, my two older brothers, their wives, and all of my nieces and nephews. We had a blast. We didn't know if that would be the last time or what. I came back to Huntsville, Alabama and kicked it with all of my friends one last time. January 22nd came around and it was time to get on the bus and head back to Nashville, Tennessee to do a final check-up. "Everything looks good, Mann. You are ready to go. Get a good night's rest. This might be the last one for a while," were the words of the doctor who conducted my physical. "Yes, sir. I will," I replied, as I walked out of his office and waited for the bus to take us back to the hotel. The next morning, I was up and my heart was pumping overtime as I got off of the bus at the airport. Here we go, ticket in hand. "Final boarding for flight to Beaufort, South Carolina!" the flight attendant called out. There was no turning back now. Sit down. Fasten the seatbelt. I was in the air. Off to boot camp...

THE DROP OFF

THE MOMENT OF TRUTH

CHAPTER 1

F or all those who didn't live it, picture this. You are on a plane, not knowing what to expect next. The captain calls for everyone to be seated and the final decent begins. There is a safe landing and out of the plane you go. Waiting for you is a man with a sign that says Parris Island Marine Recruits. Standing beside him are two other men dressed in uniform like your recruiter, but something about them looks different. Your Recruiter always smiled when he saw you. These guys don't smile. They are all about business. That's what the first few minutes were all about.

Once all who were going to boot camp got off flights from their hometowns, we lined up and got on a bus. Not a coach bus, but an old school bus. After a few minutes of silence, everyone started talking and getting to know each other. The whole time, the bus driver was quiet and smiling. The two Marines sitting right behind him were smiling now and were listening to all of the chatter going on around them. As we rode in total darkness, we saw bright lights break the darkness and noticed a sign that read "Welcome to Parris Island." Then the bus driver broke his silence.

"It's too late to turn back now, boys!"

Immediately everyone on the bus got quiet again. When the bus came to a halt, there were three additional Marines standing like the Queens guards of Buckingham Palace (just not with the big fluffy hats). The bus door opened. Ok, Robert, breathe. Then the silence was broken by one of the Marines who said:

> "Welcome to my island. You have made a decision that others dared not make. You will be pushed and challenged in ways you've never seen. You will be tested and you will want to quit. Look around at the one sitting next to you. These are the ones you will start this journey with, but who may not be there in the end. The question is, will you? Now look out my windows and you will see my yellow footprints. On my command and only then, you will get off my bus and stand on my yellow footprints. Are there any freakin' questions? Good. Now GET OFF MY FREAKIN' BUS NOW... MOVE IT! MOVE IT! WE DON'T HAVE ALL NIGHT!"

In about two full minutes, the bus had emptied. It was total chaos. Three busloads of young men were running like there was no tomorrow towards yellow painted footprints, not knowing what to think and not having time to think. All I saw and heard were those five Marines screaming and making sure they got into everyone's faces yelling, walking up and down the row. Once all "their" footprints were full, I heard the next command:

> "GET IN MY BUILDING! YOUR BUTTS (that's not the word that was used, but let's just says it rhymes with grass) BELONG TO ME NOW."

Not knowing what to think, say, or do, all I could do was move alone with the pack. What I did know is that it was too late for all of this. I just got off of a bus, a plane, and another bus. I was tired. What in the world did I sign up for? Why all the screaming? Can't this wait until the morning? Why does their breath smell like they'd been chewing on a whole box of cigarettes all night? Do you think I said any of that? NO! That's what was going on in my head, but never would it cross my lips. Sorry, I'm not about that life.

As the night/morning went on, we were put into platoons and our heads were scalped, not shaved. No, this was not a nice haircut. We were stripped of our civilian clothes and everything we brought - watches, wallets, everything. We were given the chance to call our loved ones, well one of our loved ones, to tell them that we had made it and that was all. We were issued uniforms, cammies, PT gear, tennis shoes (go fasters), and our black Cadillac's (boots). But, let me go back to what happened prior to all of this. Sorry. I got caught up in the memory.

Before we were ever issued anything, we were ordered to sit in a room. In this room one of the Marines in charge of processing talked to us about what was expected of us during boot camp. He also went on to tell us what was not allowed in "his" dear Corps. This was a recruit's chance to say what he had done illegally without anything happening to him. This was our Moment of Truth.

Enlistment into the military is contingent upon, along with other qualifications, passing a drug test. Failure to pass this test could result in you being discharged on less than honorable terms. There were two times that we received this Moment of Truth. The first was pre-boot camp while at MEPS prior to swearing into the Delayed Entry Program and at boot camp prior to being issued all of our gear and beginning the boot camp process. This "Moment of Truth" was the chance to tell what you had done that would also show up on a drug test. Here is where we had the opportunity to stand up and admit "I smoked weed last night" or "me and my friends snorted some powder and I'm still high." If you spoke up here, you were sent back home, but could still have the chance to re-enter the military after you went home and cleared your system.

14

At this time when the Marine in charge of this processing stage called for the Moment of Truth, if you had anything to report, you got up and walked to the front of the classroom to say what you had done in front of everyone. Then you got walked out and, well let's just say, you didn't participate in any other activities of boot camp.

Even though you would be sent home, you didn't have to worry about a bad conduct discharge. For the most part, you could still have another chance to clean up and come back to boot camp later. This may sound harsh, but during this Moment of Truth you were "forgiven" of what you had done and given a chance to return to training. Sounds familiar? It does to me. Even though it wasn't weed or dope, there were several men in the Bible who had to confess their sins. One really stands out to me. David had a "Moment of Truth" situation also. He had more than one, but let's just talk about the good one.

There was David, King of Israel, in full glory. During the spring of the year when he was supposed to be out with his troops, David was taking a break; walking on his rooftop when he noticed this PHAT (that's pretty hot and tempting), FINE little lady taking a bath. He asked one of his servants who she was and they gave up the name. He sent for her to come to his chambers. When she got there, he had sex with her. Not only did they have sex, but also he got her pregnant. Oh, let me remind you, this was the wife of Uriah, one of David's best soldiers.

15

When David found out that she was pregnant, he had to do something to cover his tracks, so he sent word for Uriah to return from the frontline of the war. Uriah got back to the city and David told him to go home, wash up, and relax with his wife. The next day, David found out that Uriah slept outside with the servants. With his plan in mind to have Uriah go home and sleep with his wife so that this child could be put off on him, David asked Uriah why he didn't go home. Uriah replied:

> *"The ark and Israel and Judah are staying in tents and my commander Joab and my lord's men are camped in the open country. How could I go to my house to eat and drink and make love to my wife? As surely as you live, I will not do such a thing" (2 Samuel 11:11 NIV).*

David came back with, "Ok, well, just chill here for one more day and tomorrow, I will send you back." That night, David got Uriah full and drunk. They had a good ole' time until Uriah passed out. While Uriah was asleep, David wrote a note for Joab, leader of the troops out in the field, basically telling him to put Uriah back on the frontline and to pull everyone back so that the enemy would kill him. When Uriah went back out, Joab did exactly what he was told to do and Uriah was killed. Joab then sent word back to David, telling him that what he had commanded had been done. David heard and so did Uriah's wife, Bathsheba.

After she mourned for her husband, David sent for her and they married. Don't forget that she was pregnant.

Nathan the prophet, sent by God, came to David and played the smoothest trick on him. He told a story about two men in the same city - one rich and the other poor. He told about how the rich man had huge flocks of sheep and cattle and how the poor man had nothing but one female lamb. Nathan drew David in by telling him that the poor man had bought this little lamb and raised it with his own children as a member of the family. How it was almost like a daughter to him. The story went on to mention a visitor who came to see the rich man, but he was too stingy to use his own animals to make a meal for the visitor so he went and took the poor man's only lamb and made a meal.

Oh, David went off. "Where is this man? He needs to be punished for what he has done. As a matter of fact, not only punished, but killed for this crime. But before he is killed, he must pay this poor man back four times over." Nathan told David, "Sir, you are that man." Nathan went on to tell King David the words from God. How He had made him king and given him everything he had asked for and would have given him even more. He also told David what he had done to Uriah and how now, because he had treated God with such contempt, what would happen to him and his family. How God would make trouble out of his own family and how his wives would be taken from him and given to his neighbors and everyone would see them in public.

Here was David's Moment of Truth. Here, David had to say that he had sinned against God. David was forgiven and told that he would not die for this sin, but that there would be consequences. In David's Moment of Truth, Nathan had to tell David that even though he wouldn't die, he would lose his son by Bathsheba. In losing his son, after a week of sorrow and praying that God would have mercy on the child, David went to the sanctuary and worshiped. After eating and worship, he went to his wife and comforted her and they conceived another child whom they named Solomon. We know the history of this child. He became the next King of Israel and was loved by God.

In life we are faced with Moments of Truth. Today, I want you to think of what you need to come clean with and make this the day you have a Moment of Truth. Yes, it is true that there may be consequences that we will have to live with, but we have a promise. If we tell the truth, it's not over. As a matter of fact, you can feel free.

In the Marines and in the story of David, there are things that were lost. The chance to participate in boot camp right then to the loss of a child, but that is not the end of the story. There are several persons who have gone home, gotten themselves together, and returned to boot camp to train. David lost a child, but he was able to have another son. He not only had another son, but he was the son who would take over his throne and rule the kingdom of the Israelites.

Here's your Moment of Truth. God already has the test results. Are you the one who will stand up and admit your wrongs before it's too late or will you receive a Bad Conduct Discharge from God's military?

> *"For the wages of sin is death, but the gift of God is eternal life through Jesus Christ our Lord"* *(Romans 6:23 KJV).*

I didn't have to stand up in the Marine Corps Moment of Truth, but I know I have done wrong. "Yes, God, I did it. Please forgive me of my sins. I don't want a Bad Conduct Discharge of death. Please give me another chance at eternal life."

> *"Come now, and let us reason together, saith the Lord: though your sins be as scarlet, they shall be as white as snow; though they be red like crimson, they shall be as wool." (Isaiah 1:18 KJV).*

My drug of choice was women. When I saw one, I instantly went into conquer mode. My addiction came to a head when I dated my wife (before we were married) and was still talking to other women on the side. When she found out, there was nothing I could say. I had done wrong. I lost the best thing that had ever happened to me. I lost what God promised me because He had showed me that this was the woman I was supposed to marry. In losing her, I had to deal with my own Moment of Truth.

I first had to pray and ask God for forgiveness. Not one of those elaborate prayers, but I literally had to cry out with tears, asking God for another chance at what was promised to me. I also had to ask for forgiveness from several people, including the ladies that I had been in contact with and had been sexual with. I told them that I could not continue going about life the way I had previously. I then had to beg for forgiveness from the one I loved. This didn't come easy and I hated myself for what I had done. I started out blaming others for my wrong doings. "They knew I was with her. Why did they even talk to me?" I had to come to a place where I was ready to except responsibility for my own actions. I was wrong and no one had forced me into these conversations and sex. It was all me. Once I got there, I worked and worked and worked for what I needed and what was promised to me. I had to come to a place where I was ready for God to control my actions instead of me. I allowed Him to enter my situation and take control. But the first step was admitting that I had done wrong and wanted help. Today, she is not just still my girlfriend, but my wife and my love for her is stronger than ever. Yes, it was a very tough time, but God restores.

There are many of you reading this who are struggling with drugs, sex, or alcohol and are ready to live right. Here is what I did that may help you. Pray. Not that elegant prayer you hear the elders or deacons pray at church, but have a real conversation with your Dad. Yes, Dad. This Moment of Truth is all about forgiveness. We worship and serve a God of another chance. This means we can come to Him with what we have done and ask for forgiveness. Don't get me wrong, there are penalties for doing wrong, but there is also a chance to get it right.

It is time to correct our wrongs, learn from our past mistakes, and begin to live right. Keep training in God's boot camp. This has to come from your Moment of Truth with our Heavenly Father. "Daddy, this is your son. I've done wrong. I need help." We spend so much time trying to hide the fact that we are dealing with something that we begin to believe that we can fool Him. God knows what you are fighting. Be real with Him. "Daddy, I enjoy sex. You made us to enjoy sex, but I am having sex out of the context of Your will. I know that sex outside marriage is wrong and if left up to me to make the decision, I am going to fail again. But I need you, Daddy, to take this urge away from me. Please, Daddy…" Go to Him lay and it all out. He already knows, but will not force Himself into our situations. Invite Him in and watch Him work. He can't wait to help you.

Your Moment of Truth may not be drugs or even sex, but we have all wronged someone. That someone may be your wife, family member, or co-worker. Whoever it is, you need to go to that person and ask for forgiveness. Go to your wife and make things right for wrongs that you have done. You may be thinking you were in the right, but fellas, our responsibility on this earth are to be priests and protectors of our families. But our way of showing we are protectors is all messed up. Being a protector means making it easy for your wife to come and talk to you while you LISTEN. Allow her space to feel comfortable with you. No matter how much you try to force her to feel comfortable, you will fail. This comfort comes in knowing that she won't be made to feel like her feelings don't matter. Her opinion is valid and sometimes we just have to work on not taking over the conversation or telling her how to handle a situation. She will feel protected when she has a safe place to communicate with the one she loves. That is being a protector.

It may even mean that you have to go to your children and ask for forgiveness for not being the father you know you need to be. You may have spent all your time working and bringing home the bacon while your children were home wanting their daddy to just come home and teach them how to catch a football, have tea time with them, or so they could spend time with you fixing on the house or car. Do it before it's too late. That is being a daddy.

Go to your fellow brother and apologize for being the one who started that rumor about him. Yes, it may be that you have to stand in front of what feels like a firing squad, but forgiveness is well worth it. It's time to kick all of these habits and begin anew right now. Make things right with them, whoever they may be, and stand in front of God with the promise that this is not your last

chance, but that He is giving you another chance.   Good to go…
Hit the racks fellas. Tomorrow will be a long day.

CLASS IS IN SESSION

MY GENERAL ORDERS

CHAPTER 2

LIGHTS, LIGHTS, LIGHTS!!!

Yep, that was my morning alarm clock for the next 13 weeks; early before the sun thought about coming up. What time was it? I had no clue because my watch had been taken in processing. As soon as my wake-up alarm sounded, it was all about training. Along with physical activities, we sat in classes and learned all types of information about the history of the Marine Corps and where it all began.

November 10, 1775

Tun Tavern Philadelphia, Pennsylvania

It's just like Marines to be drunk and want to fight. We learned nicknames such as:

Leatherneck

Jarhead

Teufelhunden

Devil Dog

We learned where the names came from and why Marines were called these names. We also had to learn the chain of command from the President of the United States all the way down to our squad leader. We repeated this information day in and day out. We repeated this while in class and also during formation, moving from one place to the next. We had to study our "Green Monsters," our book of everything a recruit needed to know about his dear Marine Corps. We even learned what to do with wounds in wartime and the steps to go through to assist in saving a life.

However, there was one thing that we had to know verbatim that stood out to me. It was a set of eleven (twelve, depending on who you talk to), rules that would be the basis of everything we did in the Marine Corps, standing sentry watch or working as Military Police. These rules became known as our eleven General Orders. We had to repeat them every day. These orders were etched into our brains and I can repeat them today.

"What's my General Orders?"

"Sir, this recruit's General Orders are:

1. To take charge of my post and all government property in sight.
2. To walk my post in a military manner, keeping always on the alert and observing everything that takes place within sight or hearing.
3. To report all violations of orders I am instructed to enforce.
4. To repeat all calls from post more distant from the guardhouse than my own.
5. To quit my post only when properly relieved.
6. To receive, obey, and pass on to the sentry who relieves me, all orders from the CO, OOD, and NCO of the guard only.
7. To talk to no one except in the line of duty.
8. To give the alarm in case of fire or disorder.
9. To call the Corporal of the Guard in any case not covered by instruction.
10. To salute all officers, colors, and standards not cased.
11. To be especially watchful at night and during the time of challenging, to challenge all persons on or near my post, and to allow no one to pass without proper authority.
12. I will leave this one for us Marines who can remember. If not, it starts out "To walk my post from flank to flank..."

All day, every day, this was asked of us. It was burned into our memories. These were the rules we would live by if we stayed in for one term or until retirement. This was etched into the way we thought and lived.

It reached the point where while standing sentry watch, one would automatically perform these orders without being reminded. During boot camp, we had to stand sentry watch for two hours during the night while everyone slept. Two rotation sentries walked their post, checking for any violations and questioning anyone that approached our squad bay all night, every two hours. Even in the daytime when we were on line in the bays, if someone, usually a drill instructor, came through the hatch (a door), we would yell "HATCH!" The individual would call his title out and announce himself on deck. We were always taught to watch and observe everything that was going on around us.

There were nights when Drill Instructors got bored and played "games" with us just to make sure the sentry was on his post. One Drill Instructor who was Reconnaissance Special Forces would get bored and low-crawl through the squad bay and snatch recruits out of their racks to see how long it would take the sentry to find out what was going on in the bay. It started out that he could get all the way to the end of one row before the sentry found out what was going on. Over time, the sentry would figure him out and stop him sooner. There were many nights I remember being asleep, out cold, then awakened after hitting the floor. This only made us more prepared and made us learn the general orders even more. These were our general orders.

This part of training reminds me of Moses and the Children of Israel. We know the story. Moses, born a slave, raised in the palace of Egypt, lived in the desert only to come back to Egypt because God said so. Yeah, *that* Moses. Let me get to the good part. When the children of Israel reached the Desert Sinai and were at the foot of Mount Sinai, God called Moses up to the mountain and told him to get the people ready because He (God) had something to say. He also told Moses to tell the people to wash their clothes and get ready, but not to touch the mountain, or they would die. Moses went down and passed the word to the people and they began to prepare for what was about to happen. Three days later, the mountain became smoky with thunder, lightning, and a very loud trumpet blast. Everyone was shaken and Moses gathered them at the foot of the mountain.

During a previous conversation between God and Moses, God called Moses up to the mountain and told him to bring Aaron with him. Then God spoke:

> *"I am the Lord your God, who brought you out of the land of Egypt, out of the house of bondage" (Exodus 20:2 NIV).*

Then God went on to give His ten General Orders:

1. *"You shall have no other gods before me.*

2. *You shall not make for yourself any image in the form of anything in the heavens above or the earth beneath or in the waters below. You shall not bow down to them or worship them for I, the Lord your God, am a jealous God, punishing the children for the sins of the parents to the third and fourth generation of those who hate me, but showing love to a thousand generations of those who love me and keep my commandments.*

3. *You shall not misuse the name of the Lord your God for the Lord will not hold anyone guiltless who misuses his name.*

4. *Remember the Sabbath day by keeping it holy. Six days you shall labor and do all your work, but the 7th day is a Sabbath to the Lord your God. On it you shall not do any work neither you nor your sons or daughters nor your male or female servant nor your animals, nor any foreigner residing in your towns. For in six days the Lord made the heavens and the earth, the sea, and all that is in them, but he rested on the 7th day. Therefore the Lord blessed the Sabbath day and made it holy.*

5. *Honor your father and your mother, so that you may live long in the land that Lord your God is giving you.*

6. *You shall not murder.*

7. *You shall not commit adultery.*

8. *You shall not steal.*

9. *You shall not give false testimony against your neighbor.*

10. *You shall not covet your neighbor's house. You shall not covet your neighbor's wife, or his male or female servant his ox or donkey or anything that belongs to your neighbor" (Exodus 20:3-17 NIV).*

We wanted to be Marines, so we made sure that we followed EVERY general order. That is what we call them, but *your* job may call its rules Standard Operating Procedures. Others may call them by-laws. Whatever they are called, wherever you are, if you want to continue working there, you must follow ALL of the rules. Most places where you work require you to sign that you have received, read, and agree with these rules along with the consequences of breaking any of them. If you are a student, your teacher distributes a course syllabus that includes the teacher's expectations. It informs you of assignment due dates and what percentage of your grade comes from papers, assignments, and tests. With all of these types of General Orders, we agree to the terms and if we break ONE of these rules, it is subject to disciplinary action, so we keep ALL of them.

Years after enlisting in the Marine Corps, I prided myself in thinking that I kept all of God's General Orders until one day I really started thinking about what I was doing. I had several gods that took the place of the one true God. The main god I had was smoking marijuana. I had an "at least five blunts-a-day" habit. I woke up in the morning and smoked, took a break from work and smoked, went home and smoked to relieve myself of the stresses of the day. I smoked one to eat, smoked at least one just because I wanted to get high again, and ended my night with smoking one to go to bed. Why do I call this a god? Well, I didn't think I could deal with the pressures of the day, so I smoked – went to my god and laid my stress at its feet. I did this just like some of us go down to the altar and leave our burdens at the God's feet. The difference is, I always felt as though I had to continue smoking so as not to feel any pain.

It started out with just one blunt and I liked how it made me feel. I would not have to worry about anything during the time that I was high. Then it got to the point where I was always worried and didn't know why. So I smoked more and more. I began spending more money to worship my god. The more money I spent, the worse I felt. I began stressing about how to take care of bills. God began to show me that He was way more powerful than any god I had. He took me from being "the man" in my community to nothing. I had no other option but to reach out to whom I already knew was there. *"Daddy, if you can help me and show me that you are more powerful than this weed, I will trust You and You only."* I stood on that promise and God started showing me things that I could not see while worshiping my little god. He began opening up doors to better jobs and put money in my pocket. He took me right back to His general orders. *"Thou shalt have no other gods before me" (Exodus 20:3 KJV).* I put that weed down for good and began spending time with the only true God.

Question, fellas. Are you keeping ALL of God's General Orders or are you only keeping the ones that fit into your life? The ones that feel right to you? God's General Orders are set up so that we can show love. The first four General Orders are about our love towards God and the last six are orders about love towards our fellow man. We may not have gods that we put over God, but are you looking at your neighbors driving that brand new Lexus and killing yourself to try and keep up? That is coveting. We may love our parents and may take care of them day in and day out, but are we resting on the seventh day of the week like God commanded us to? Remember the Sabbath day. We may not be picking up that .45 and blasting someone in the chest, but are we using that weapon called the tongue to kill our fellow brothers. That is bearing false witness against your neighbor.

We are given these commandments to show the true meaning of love. There are many rules that we keep daily. Rules for our jobs, traffic rules, and even rules to live in certain areas.

We are sure to keep these rules. We keep them so that we will have a place to live, work, or the right to drive a particular vehicle. If we break these rules, there is a possibility that we will not have any of those things. We do not go to work and tell the boss that we are only going to follow a few of the rules. While some of us do not do this, you get my point. If we did that, we would surely be shown the front door by security or maybe even called and told not to come in… EVER… We do not tell the police officer, "Well, I didn't think that speeding rule applied to me; I'm just here to abide by driving on the correct side of the road rule and nothing else." No, we make sure to keep those rules.

Question. Why do we break our necks to pay so much attention to worldly General Orders, but put God's General Orders to the side? Don't you think God deserves more respect for all of his General Orders than the military, government, or work? Men, if we start standing up for what we believe and obeying God's General Orders, our families and friends will follow. Our lives will be in union with God's will and He will bless everything that we touch. If you don't believe me, repeat His General Orders. It says that He will show mercy and love to the ones that love Him. Next time we hear God ask us to repeat our General Orders, do it. Learn them. Be able to repeat them and have them so etched into your memory that you just do them without even thinking about it. It's something to think about. I'm just saying… Good to Go?

P.T.

THE
OBSTACLE
COURSE

CHAPTER 3

"GET OUT MY RACKS! LET'S GO, MOVE IT MOVE IT! OK YOU HAVE 3, 2, 1! YOU'RE DONE, YOU'RE DONE! GET OUT MY SQUAD BAY AND GET ON MY PT FIELD NOW!"

"AYE SIR?"

"AYE SIR."

"OH NO AYE SIR?"

"AYE SIR."

Yes, physical training. PT good for me, good for you. Physical training was a huge part of boot camp. They had to "break you down to build you up" mentally and most of all, physically. We always did some kind of physical training. Training from the PT table in the mornings, which consisted of exercises, was completed on four counts. That means, whatever the total number of exercises we had to do, we did double. *1, 2, 3, ONE.* Various exercises included pushups, lunges, pull-ups, and everything in between. This table also consisted of runs from 1.5 miles to 5 miles on various surfaces. One of my favorite runs was called the Moto Run.

On this run, we lined up in battalion formation and the company or battalion officer along with the Sergeants Major would lead. These were fun, as we would hear our drill instructors call out cadence. If you had some "soul," you might be called out to lead cadence. On these runs, you could be a motivator and grab the platoon colors and run around the whole battalion. Physical training did not stop with the table; we also would get "smoked" all day. Now, before you call all the congressmen in the United States and tell them you heard me say we were smoking, let me explain.

Getting smoked was physical discipline. For punishment, we would have to exercise instead of being physically punished. Push-ups, sit-ups, mountain climbers and anything else our Drill Instructors could think of. This "smoke session" happened in the squad bays, classrooms, on the parade deck, or in our lovely sand pits. Ahhhh, the sand pits with our favorite pets - sand fleas. I don't know what the Hollywood Marines out in San Diego had to go through, but Parris Island Marines - *THIRD BATTALION MARINES* - got smoked in sand pits.

To explain sand pits, if you have never seen one, they look like playground sand boxes. If you lived it and are like me, you will never look at a playground sand box the same ever again. This is where I got in the best shape of my life. It seemed like I lived in these pits after getting in trouble to being a Squad Leader and having to get smoked with or for one of the recruits in my squad. Like every Marine that lived in that Squad Bay, there is a lot of my sweat, blood, and tears left in those pits. Oh, and don't let the DI's *really* get mad, we would have to visit every sand pit in the area. That was what we called "island hopping." Sand pits and sand fleas... But, let me get back on topic. I got lost with all of the talk about sand pits and smoking where I almost forgot the other physical training event. It was my favorite - the Obstacle Course; O Course for short.

I will never forget as we marched up to an adult playground with ropes, logs, and monkey bars. Little did we know that this course would eat us alive. There were 14 obstacles and they were nothing to play with.

1. The Dirty Name
2. Run, Jump, Swing
3. The Confidence Climb, also known as the Stairway to Heaven
4. The Inclining Wall
5. Reverse Climb
6. Cargo Net
7. Monkey Bridge
8. Slide for Life
9. The Tough One "A-frame"
10. Weaver
11. Balance Logs
12. Arm Stretcher
13. Wall Climb
14. The Skyscraper

The first six or so are just a quick run through, but further into the course, you hit the monkey bridge, and my favorite, the Slide for Life. I will park at this obstacle for a minute... Let me explain.

Let me take you to boot camp for a minute. First, I had to climb up a log ladder. When I got to the top, a rope was suspended over a dirty, (I don't know what was in it), jet-black water. From what I could see, bugs hovered over the water and dirt and grass was in it. Urban legend was that alligators had been seen in it. I never saw one, but I took their word for it. Once I was at the top, I had to lie face down on the rope with one leg dangling off of the rope and pull myself down the rope. WAIT, it gets better. A few feet down the rope, I had to flip over, holding onto the rope and continue with a reverse pull down the rope. Easy, right? Wait, THEN, I had to twist around and slide down, upside-down, now feet first the rest of the way. At any time, if I could not make any turn or became tired, I would have to hang until the Drill Instructor told me to drop. Yes, drop. They tell me that there is a net over that black water so the recruits won't get wet or sick from being cold or from whatever may have been in there, but when I went through, there was no net. There was nothing but time and space between me dangling on this little rope and the cold, mucky, muddy pool of crud.

I have to say that I could not make it all the way down the rope, so here I was at a dead hang, waiting for my Drill Instructor to tell me to drop. When I was finally told to drop, I instantly snapped to attention as I fell and sang the Marine Corps Hymn until I hit the water. This obstacle took me out. Remember, I went to boot camp in January and this was mid-February. Yeah, the water still cold. Funny, as I am writing this and I am making excuses, thinking about the time I said that if it had have been March or April, it would have made a difference... HA! No, I don't think so. Cold, wet, tired, and feeling defeated, I still had to climb the A-frame, complete the arm stretcher, and finish up the course with the skyscraper. I could not give up. I had to keep on pushing. Not to mention, I had a Drill Instructor in my face telling me to:

"Suck it up Mann; let's go! What, you're a quitter?"

"NO SIR!"

"Good, then keep it moving!"

After finally completing the O Course, it was weird, but I felt good. I forgot about the obstacle that almost made me quit. I forgot about my wet cammies, the dirty water, and feeling like I failed. I did it. I finished. I got over the obstacle and looking back, it wasn't that bad. Actually, it *was* bad, but I learned techniques, and at that time, I said if I got the chance to do it again, I knew what to do and learned from my mistakes and would KILL THIS COURSE. Well, guess what? Later in training, I hit the same O Course. Just as before, I breezed through the first part of the course. When I reached the infamous Slide for Life, everything came right back to me - how I couldn't make it the last time. And yes, that cold water was still below me, but I had to keep on going. I looked at it, climbed the ladder, climbed onto the rope, made the first turn and kept on going. I reached the part of the obstacle that had taken me out the last time and...I made it through. *"Yes! Oh yeah! Oh yeah! Who's the man...?"* Even with my mental victory, I still had that same Drill Instructor screaming at me, but this time he was yelling, "Good to go Mann! You didn't get wet this time! Now, GET TO MOVING; YOU STILL GOT THE REST TO DO!" Man, those DI's never gave up.

All this talk about obstacles makes me think about Joshua. Joshua, born a slave in Egypt, was the leader who took over after Moses died. Joshua was the man who brought the children of Israel into the Promised Land. After crossing over the Jordan River, there was something in his way; an obstacle course, if you don't mind me calling it that. This obstacle was greater and stronger than the children of Israel. This obstacle had walls up to the sky. This obstacle was named Jericho. Joshua knew that God had promised this land to the children of Israel (hence the name Promised Land), but had to discover God's plan to overtake this obstacle.

To acquire intelligence on the city, Joshua sent a few Reconnaissance Marines in to check it out. When they made it inside the city, they linked up with Rahab, a local prostitute. The king received word that the spies were in town, so he sent Rahab a Facebook message. A Facebook message may be a bit of a stretch, but follow me. The king sent word to Rahab, telling her to give up the spies. She hid them and sent a reply back to the king that they had been there, but had left at dusk through the gates before they had closed. The soldiers would need to go quickly to catch them. Rahab asked the spies to save her and her household and with a promise from the men, she let them down the wall in a basket. When the spies got back to camp, they reported to Joshua. After crossing the Jordan, Joshua went out by himself. While walking, he saw a man with a sword. Joshua asked, "Are you for us or against us?" The man answered, "Neither…" Then the man introduced himself as the Commander of the Lord's Army. The CO went on to tell Joshua that this obstacle would be no problem and gave him his orders.

> "March around the city once with all the armed men. Do this for six days. Have seven priests carry trumpets of rams' horn in front of the ark. On the seventh day, march around the city seven times with the priests blowing the trumpet. When you hear them sound a loud blast on the trumpet, have the whole army give a loud shout, then the walls of the city will collapse and the army will go up, everyone straight in" (Joshua 6:3-5 NIV).

Joshua went back and told the people what to do. He also told them that when the city became theirs, to burn EVERYTHING and kill EVERYBODY except Rahab and her household. They were also told to put all of the silver and gold into the treasury for the Lord. Day one: "FORWARD, MARCH..." without saying anything. Days two, three, four, five, and six were to be the same thing. Day seven: six times around the city silently and on the seventh time, when they heard the horns blast, they started screaming. What do you know? The walls came tumbling down. The children of Israel went in and finished doing what God had told them to do. All EXCEPT for Mr. Achan. There always has to be one, right?

Once the walls had fallen down, Joshua sent spies to do some snooping and pooping into the next city, Ai. The spies came back and told Joshua that the city would be easy because they only needed to send about two to three thousand men to fight. No need sending the whole army. They determined that it was small and they could take it easily. So, the children of Israel took a small company of soldiers up to Ai, but they were run out of there something terrible. The rest of the children of Israel were straight up scared. Joshua ripped his clothes and cried out God, "Why? What's the deal? You mean we have come this far to fail?"

> *"The Lord said to Joshua. Stand up! What are you doing down on your face?" (Joshua 7:10 NIV)*

God went on to tell Joshua that Israel had sinned. Someone took what He'd told them to destroy. Long story short, Joshua found out that it was Achan. Joshua took Achan, his entire family, everything he owned, and what he had taken from Jericho, even the cats and dogs, and stoned and burned them/it all. Once this was taken care of, God said, "Don't be afraid. Take the whole army again to Ai and I will be with you." Joshua did this and completed the course. Not only did he take Ai, but he also took out several more cities. The Israelites fell off the "Slide for life," got wet and dirty, but had to keep going. They finished what God had for them to do. Even though they failed the first time, they got another chance to show that they had learned from their mistakes. By depending on God completely, they finished on top. Once they had tackled that obstacle, they had more to do and they had to finish.

Now, if you have not caught on so far, let me toss you a small hint. I am going to tell you about what I have had to go through in life. My testimonies are not for me to keep to myself. I have been through a lot of things in my lifetime and I know God has told me to share the lessons I have learned with someone. My bible says: *"And they overcame him by the blood and the Lamb, and by the word of their testimony"* (*Revelation 12:11 KJV*).

Who am I to try to fight the devil by myself? We are a team. I may never meet you in person, but we are here to help each other. Something I have gone through may help you. This may encourage you to help someone who may come to you about something you have been through. This is an O Course. I had no problem going through whatever it may have been. When it came to my Slide for Life, it was time to listen to someone else who was going through the same things I had been through. I failed them. I would listen to them and jump on the band wagon of "Dang, that's messed up! I hope things get better for you." I was afraid to tell my story and how I overcame.

I am a man and typically, we (men) don't talk. We just don't do that, right? Wrong. This is a misconception of men today. The moment we feel ourselves talking about what we have been through or what we are going through, we are taught that this is unmanly. We are raised watching our fathers never express when they are down or feeling like they can't make it anymore. We are raised to "suck it up" and "take it like a man." When we are hurting inside and have nowhere else to go, we release sexually. This is my chance to get back on the Slide for Life.

I am going to be honest, open, and transparent. Why? Not so you can sit back and say how much I have had to endure, but because God has placed it on my heart to care for men. He needs for us to stand back up and put on the mantle that he has ordained us as men to don. We need to be the men of our families again and take care of our children as men prior to us did. We also need to correct the misconception of men in the homes. God has given us all of the tools we need to succeed in life. Now it is on us to believe that His training is true and to go out and do. This is what God has called me to do. He has called me to reach out and touch whoever is in need of healing from my Daddy. This is my second chance to complete my Slide for Life. With the lessons I have learned and the opportunities I have been given, I will do what has been asked of me.

How many of us can say this about ourselves? We will hit that bump in the road of life and start saying, "God I can't do this. I failed. I'm no good." Then you'll hear God tell you, "Keep on going. Change some things and learn from your mistakes. It's ok. Stand up! What are you doing down there?" When we get up, we will see that we have to face the same O Course of our lives once again.

Did you correct what was wrong? Have you learned from the first time? I did and am still learning. Just like on the O Course and in the story of Joshua, we are not finished yet; we have to complete it. We have to stand up, dust ourselves off, face the obstacle, and defeat it in the name of Jesus. Once you have gone through it, move on. Just because you cleared that obstacle doesn't mean that you are finished. Keep moving. Keep going. Finish… Good to go?

A NEW NAME

A NEW WAY TO TALK

CHAPTER 4

Now when I got to boot camp, I had no clue that even my way of talking would change. The names I called certain things prior to reaching boot camp, I began calling them something different. Even now that I am out of the military, I still find myself calling things certain names based on what I learned while in the Marines. If I were talking about going up to the top floor of someplace, I would simply say "upstairs." Going down, I would say "downstairs." But, NOOOO! Now I say that I'm going "topside" or "down below." When I get sleepy, I "go to bed." In the Marines, we "hit the rack." When I have to pee, I "go to the bathroom." This has turned into "going to the head." Water fountains became scuttlebutts as did gossip; looking out of the window became looking through a porthole;

floors became decks; right became known as starboard and left was known as port. Walls are referred to as bulkheads and even walking up behind someone went from "excuse me" to "by you leave." Just in case you grew up not calling older men and women sir and ma'am, you had to get used to it. Every time I opened my mouth, it had to begin with Sir or Ma'am. The list goes on and on and on as to what I now call things, thanks to the Marines and what I was taught in boot camp.

This new way of talking was etched into my memory by repetition and the aid of physical assistance. The words I, me, and my first name were put in a bag mailed back to Huntsville, Alabama. One of the main reasons for the sand pits was if I slipped up and used them. If I needed something, I asked in third person. "Sir, this recruit needs…" I learned many things about the other recruits, but one thing we hardly knew were their first names. My first name was Recruit and my last name was Mann. The drill instructors names were Sr. or Jr. Drill Instructor, Staff Sergeant, and whatever their last names were followed by Sir. That is what you had better call them or a smoking session would result. Trust me, we got it wrong a lot and when we did, we paid for it. I'm not mentioning any names, but there have been recruits who were lifted off the floor for disrespectful answers. Even with the "no touching" rule in place, there were a few exceptions to those rules. There was no "laying of hands" on the recruits, so parents reading this, don't worry; your children are in good hands. We were in good hands, literally, but yeah, anyway, back to my story. There were changes in the way we talked and changes in our names.

How are you going to take my name away from me? Growing up, there were two names I was called; my nickname, Bobby and my government name, Robert. To this day, my friends and family call me Bobby. When I was in trouble, I got "ROBERT LEE MANN, JR!" I knew what was up then. Now, that had changed. All of a sudden, if another recruit wanted to call me by my first name, it was a problem. I dared not ask that question, but they knew we were going to ask it, so here is the logic behind it.

"There is freakin' two things that keep us freakin' separated as men, you understand? Freakin' your first names and what freakin' color you are. There are a lot of Smiths in the world, but only a few John Smiths and even less black, freakin' John Smiths. So let's freakin' level the field. Everybody's name will be your freakin' rank and there is no different color or race. The only race here is freakin' green. Either you are light green or dark green. You understand?"

Yep, that is the way the drill instructors talked. They used a lot of freakin's and doggone's and you get the picture. There were more choice words as well but we will keep it rated PG for now. As recruiters, we even started freakin' doggone talking like that. It was freakin' doggone everything. This made sense to us. We were the same; we were green recruits; and we were equal. We weren't Tom, a great hunter from Tennessee; street smart Jamal from New York, or Sam from Florida, who was an A student, had parents who were well off, and had a nice ride. We were all the same. We all had the same dreams of being a member of Uncle Sam's Misguided Children (USMC).

There was someone in the Bible who had his name changed, not by a Marine Drill Instructor or anything like that, but by God. Abraham, son of Terah of Ur, was spoken to by God several times and was told that he and his offspring would be blessed for years and years to come. But Abraham was not Abraham from the beginning. Abraham's official government name was Abram. Abram moved from Ur to Heran and then to Canaan by the age of 75. He, his wife Sarai, and his nephew Lot, lived together. They even moved to Egypt for a while because of the drought. In Egypt, Abram said to his wife, "I know you look good and they are going to fall in love with you, so tell them that you are my sister to save my life."

When they arrived in Egypt, Pharaoh called for Sarai and she lived with Pharaoh as Abram's sister. For this, Abram was saved and taken care of. He was given sheep, cattle, donkeys, female and male servants. Then God struck the house of Pharaoh with sickness. When Pharaoh found out that this sickness was a result of Sarai being with him, he came to Abram and said, "What have you done to me? Why didn't you tell me Sarai was your wife? Bro, look, take everything I have given to you and go. Take your wife, too." When they left, God came to Abram again and told him that he and his offspring would be blessed. Remember, Abram was up in age. He was older than 80 years and his wife could not bear children. What was all this talk about offspring?

Abram took things into his own hands and hooked up with one of Sarai's servants. Wait, Sarai hooked him up with one of her servants. Really? I know, right. Who does that? Anyway, Sarai's slave, Hagar, slept with Abram and she became pregnant. At 86 years old, Abram had a child named Ishmael. Then God came to Abram at the age of 99 and reminded him of His covenant regarding his offspring. Then, here we go, God told Abram:

> "No longer will you be called Abram. Your name
> will be Abraham for I will have made you a father
> of many nations" (Genesis 17:4-5 NIV).

God went on to tell Abraham what every man has/should have to go through – circumcision. Yep....snip-snip. That's not all. God also told Abram, oh, I mean, Abraham:

> "As for Sarai, your wife, you are no longer to call
> her Sarai. Her name will be Sarah. I will bless her

and will surely give you a son by her" (Genesis 17:15-16 NIV).

Yo, this tripped Abraham out. He fell down laughing like, "Really, God? I mean, I know you know everything, but You *do* remember that I am 100 and Sarah is 90, right? But You are going to give us a child?" Long story short, God blessed Abraham and Sarah with a son, Isaac. God changed his name as a constant reminder of the covenant He had made with him.

The world gives us several names outside of our government names given to us at birth. Some of these names are to put us in categories such as thug, addict, deadbeat, and loser. Some people are called pimp, player, hustler, rock star, and the list goes on. All of these names and others are based on the situations that we are in. I am so glad that our Heavenly Father also has a name for us. His name is not based on the *situation* that we are in right now, but based on *who* we are.

> *"He, who has an ear, let him hear what the Spirit says to the churches. To him who overcomes, I will give some of the hidden manna to eat. And I will give him a white stone, and on that stone a new name written which on one knows except him who receives it" (Revelation 2:17 NKJV).*

I cannot wait until I can hear God say my name. I believe there will be a change, but until then, we have to be reminded that while the world may call us one thing, we must remember that there is a name that God the Father calls us right now - Child. We must act like His children. One thing the Marines could not or did not take was my last name. No matter how many times I was promoted or my "first name" changed because of the rank or position I held, who I was could not be taken away. That stood for something. That stood for who I represented - my family. I wanted to be a Marine, but I was already a Mann. Participating in and completing boot camp, I gave respect to everyone that has ever had that name. As a man, my first name could be taken and changed to my rank, but my last name, to me, meant that was who I am. I am in this for everyone who is a Mann, from African-American to German; from my father, Pastor Robert Mann Sr., to my sons, Donovan and Robert Mann. This was something to be proud of, like being called a son of God. What name do you want to be known by? If you are like me, I cannot wait to get to heaven, sit under my heavenly Father, and hear Him call my name and tell me how proud He is to be called my Father. That is what I am living for. What about you? Good to go…

DOWN RANGE

THIS IS MY RIFLE

CHAPTER 5

I n the Marine Corps, after boot camp, I also was trained in a special skill. My Military Occupation Specialty (MOS) was 3051/3047 Supply and Logistics (Box kicker). In boot camp, we were all trained as basic riflemen. An M16 A2 service rifle with 5.56 mm rounds; 8.79 lbs. fully loaded; maximum effective range: area target - 2,684.8 ft. (800 m), point target - 1804 ft. (550 m.); muzzle velocity - 2800 ft. (853 m) per second; and magazine capacity - 30 rounds. This was to be my best friend and would accompany me when I needed it. I named it and got to know it because it belonged to me. If I took care of my rifle, it would take care of me. I had to keep it clean or it would not fire. Along with all of this, I had to get to know the Rifleman's Creed.

"This is my rifle. There are many like it, but this one is mine. My rifle is my best friend. It is my life. I must master it as I must master my life. My rifle, without me, is useless. Without my rifle, I am useless. I must fire my fire true. I must shoot straighter than my enemy who is trying to kill me. I must shoot him before he shoots me, I will...

My rifle and myself know that what counts in the war is not the rounds we fire, the noise of our burst, nor the smoke we make. We know that it is the hits that count. We will hit...

My rifle is human even as I, because it is my life. Thus, I will learn it as a brother. I will learn its weakness, its strengths, its parts, its accessories, its sights, and its barrel. I will even guard it against the ravages of weather and damage as I will even guard my legs, my arms, my eyes, and my head against damage. I will keep my rifle clean and ready. We will become part of each other. We will...

Before God, I swear this creed. My rifle and myself are the defenders of my country. We are the masters of our enemy. We are the saviors of my life

So be it until victory is America's and there is no enemy, but peace."

-Major General William H. Rupertus

This was the creed regarding my lightweight, magazine-fed, gas-operated, air-cooled, shoulder-fired weapon. Please remember that this was not a gun; this was my rifle. I had to learn the parts of my rifle: upper receiver, lower receiver, bolt, and chamber group. We had to practice disassembling our rifles in less than 30 seconds and reassembling it within 45 seconds. We had to know what to do for rifle inspection. There were several tests to take as well as we practiced carrying it in several positions. We had to do all of this before we were handed a round to fire down range. These were the safety rules:

1. Treat every weapon as if it is loaded.
2. Never point a weapon at anything you do not intent to shoot.
3. Keep your finger straight and off of the trigger until you are ready to fire.
4. Keep the weapon on safe until you intend to fire.

I had to learn what to do if my rifle jammed.

Immediate Action: Tap, Rack, Bang

Remedial Action: S.P.O.R.T.S -- **S**eek cover. **P**ull the charging handle to the rear and attempt to lock the bolt to the rear. **O**bserve for a round or brass to be ejected and take appropriate action to clear stoppage. **R**elease the bolt. **T**ap the forward assist. **S**ight and attempt to fire.

While learning all of this, I had to prepare my body for the four firing positions. Standing was no problem as we stood all of the time. It was the sitting that I had problems with. But, I had to get my body used to sitting in a cross-legged position for hours at a time. I had to learn how to control my breathing and keeping my eyes open when we were shooting. With all of that practice, I could now hit the range.

We practiced and displayed our skills. We were taught loading, unloading, and breath control. Not only did I fire my rifles, I had to "pull pits" or "pull the targets." This was cool. I would be under the bunker and would hear the round hit the target. You could hear it tumble in the air. This was something that I really cannot explain; it is one of those "you had to be there moments." All of my Marines know what I am talking about. It sends chills through my body just thinking about it.

On the range, recruits who were used to hunting had to change their thoughts and if you had never fired a weapon, either your nerves were wrecked or you were very excited or both. This week, I had the biggest smile on my face. There were recruits that wanted that expert badge and then there were the ones who just wanted to pass. I was the marksman. A score of 190 paid the bills. The range occurred around week 5 and 6 and we had been yelled at, smoked, always on the move, and tired. The range was where we could get some of that frustration off of our chests. It was just my rifle, locked in down range and me. That target was the enemy - who or whatever that may have been. With all of that testosterone running around, we had rules. We had to have them. At the end of the day we had to show our rifle chambers and clips as clear. We also had to empty our pockets, pat down, check everywhere, and repeat:

"Sir, this recruit has no brass, trash, or anything to report at this time."

Why, you say? We were dealing with real live ammo. No dummies or blanks. It was the real thing. All week, we would snap in, align our sights, and fire from 200, 300, and 500 meters from prone, sitting, kneeling, and standing positions. I got burned by hot brass and had ringing in my ears, but this was weapons training. These were great times.

I'd like to think that David had something like a rifleman's creed as well. Yes, David, slayer of Goliath. Good ole' David. He was the last son of Jesse. Remember him? God spoke to Samuel and told him to go and anoint the new king of Israel, and this king would come from the house of Jesse. When Samuel arrived with the sacrifice that God had told him to bring, Samuel invited Jesse and his sons, along with the elders of Bethlehem, to the sacrifice. Upon their arrival, Samuel started looking at Jesse's sons. One by one, he looked at them and each time, the answer from God was "No." Seven boys passed by Samuel. He then looked at Jesse and said, "These all your boys?" Jesse replied that he had another one who was out tending sheep. Samuel said, "Well, what are you waiting for? Bring him to me. I will wait."

When David got there, he was glowing with health, bright-eyed and good-looking. God told Samuel to get up because this was the one. God filled him instantly. At the same time, God's spirit left Saul, the current king of Israel, and he began to have a foul mood. His men told him they would get someone to play music to calm him down. As a matter fact, they knew just the person. Jesse had a son who could PLAY. Brave little dude and don't look too bad either. Saul was like, "Good. Go get him."

When David arrived and played, Saul made him one of his closest men. He made him his main man. Saul sent an "instant message" to Jesse saying that David was going to stay there and he thanked Jesse. Every time Saul felt bad, David played and lifted his spirits. Well, the Israelites and the Philistines had beef and one day they were standing on opposite hilltops ready to fight. This was no rap east coast/west coast battle; this was a real live "let's get it on" fight.

Out from the Philistine camp stepped this big, ten-foot "swole" giant with pounds and pounds of armor and a bronze sword. Big Goliath came out and started calling out the Israelites.

> "Send me your toughest fighter. If he beats me, no, kills me, the Philistines will become your slaves. If I kill him, you all will be our slaves. What's up? Which one of you all is ready?"

When the Israelites, along with Saul, heard this they clammed up. They was "skurred"… This went on every day for about 40 days. One day, Jesse told David to take his three brothers something to eat, make sure that they were alright, and come back to let him know what was going on with them, Saul, and the war. When he got there, he said, "What's up?" to his brothers. While he was talking to them, guess what happened? Yep, Goliath came out talking all that junk. I can just imagine some of the Israelites saying;

> "Did you hear that the dude that kills him would have it made? He will get money and clothes. Man, I heard they might even get the king's daughter as a wife."

Then another soldier chimed in;

> "Go 'head, bro. Gone out there then."

> "Man, I'm good. I'm straight."

David overheard some of what these men were saying and was like, "Wait, what will the man get again?" In the middle of him asking this question, his older brother stepped in with:

"What are you doing? Boy, go back to your little sheep. This is grown folks' business out here. You're just here to get a good seat so that you can put this bloody battle on YouTube."

Ok, I know instant messages and YouTube weren't around back then, but you get the picture.

David replied:

"Bro, what are you talking about? All I did was ask a question."

David walked off and went to check on Saul. When he got there, he said, "Let me fight this dude." Saul looked at him and said, "Come on, man. You're too little to fight." They went back and forth for a while with David telling Saul about killing lions that came up while he was tending sheep.

"If God helped me kill a lion, I know I can kill this Philistine pig."

Since no one else was stepping up, Saul gave in and put David in all of his armor. When David tried to walk, he couldn't even move.

"Saul, Sir, Master, with all due respect, (Marines loved saying that to officers as this was like asking permission to speak freely; you could say whatever you wanted), I'm gonna take this off. I'm not used to all of this."

David took it all off, picked up his shepherd's staff, picked up five smooth stones, and put them in his pocket. He checked for his sling, his rock-fed service rifle, and started walking. When Goliath saw him, he started tripping.

"Man really? You all send me this red, apple-cheeked, peach-fuzzed head little dude? What, I'm a dog that you come at me with this stick? I'm about to make you buzzard food. LOL. As matter of fact, food for the field mice."

"Then said David to the Philistine, Thou comest to me with a sword, and with a spear, and with a shield: but I come to thee in the name of the LORD of hosts, the God of the armies of Israel, whom thou hast defied. This day will the LORD deliver thee into mine hand; and I will smite thee, and take thine head from thee; and I will give the carcases of the host of the Philistines this day unto the fowls of the

air, and to the wild beasts of the earth; that all the earth may know that there is a God in Israel" (1 Samuel 17:45-46 KJV).

As David started walking towards Goliath, I can just hear David going through his own Rifleman/Sling creed.

"This is my sling. There are many like it, but this one is mine. My sling is my best friend. It is my life. I must master it as I must master my life. My sling, without me, is useless. Without my sling, I am useless. I must swing my sling true. I must shoot this rock straighter than my enemy who is trying to kill me. I must strike him before he hits me I will…

My sling and myself know that what counts in the war is not the number of stones I use, the sound it makes, nor all the trash talk we do. We know that it is the hits that count. We will hit…

My sling is human even as I because it is my life. Thus. I will learn it as a brother. I will learn its weakness, its strengths, its parts its accessories, its sights, and its barrel. I will even guard it against the ravages of weather and damage as I will even guard my legs, my arms, my eyes and my head against damage. I will keep my sling clean and ready. We will become part of each other. We will…

As God is my witness to this creed. My sling and myself are the defenders of my country. We are the masters of this uncircumcised giant. As God is the Savior of my life.

Now, let's get it on…"

Goliath started towards David. David took off towards Goliath. David reached into his pocket, pulled out a stone (5.56mm round), loaded his sling, swung it, let it go, and hit Goliath smack in the forehead. I like to call this "one shot, one kill." Goliath stopped in his tracks and fell face down in the dirt. The rest is history.

I have had some Goliaths to slay in my life. In some instances, I acted like the men of the Israelite army and allowed what seemed to be larger than life problems have control of my life and send me running. One of the Goliaths was drinking. Yep, I used this along with smoking marijuana to try and hide my sorrows. Drinking was a huge part of my life. I couldn't pass a store without looking up and seeing my Goliath talking bad to me. Calling me a loser; reminding me that I was so deep in debt and worthless that I might as well drink. In this weak state, I would find myself pulling in to pick up at least a six-pack and/or something stronger. Once, I got home, bottles would crack, tops would pop, and I would, as my middle brother said all of the time before he passed, try to find my sorrows at the bottom of the bottle.

Every day I felt as though I needed something cold and strong to end my day of work. My bottle was my creed, but it was a creed that I knew would end in destruction. I saw no other way to cope. Then I picked up another weapon. This weapon, along with help from experts, replaced my bottle. I began to see that, yes, I would fail every day, but that was me trying to fight this Goliath on my own. I could not do this by myself. I needed help.

What was that weapon? Well, I'm glad you asked. It was and still is the Bible. I started reading promises in the bible and saw my Goliath of selfishness get stopped right in its tracks. There are so many promises in this book. If you give a liberal tithe and offering, God will give back to you (Malachi 3:10). If you are tired, God tells you to give it to Him (Matthew 11:28). If you have lost someone close to you and are just sad, God promises that joy will come (Psalms 30:5). There are so many 5.56mm rounds already preloaded in this weapon that there is no reason why you shouldn't carry it around. Oh, and here is the good part - God has already won the war. Ok, you just missed your shouting opportunity so I will give it to you like this:

> *"For God so loved the world that he gave his only begotten Son, that whosoever believeth in him*

should not perish, but have everlasting life" (John 3:16 KJV).

What about us? I know we don't carry round an M16-A2 rifle or even a sling, but we do have a weapon that God has issued to us. His Word. In this Word, there are many rounds that will allow us to defeat the enemy. We can read story after story of how the devil was defeated. But, the first thing we have to do is pick it up. In some cases, we have to dust if off. Next, OPEN it and begin reading the promises that God has spoken. There are words of encouragement for the "War on Depression." Words of love for your neighbor to help in the "Battle on Haterade Hill." Guess what? God has even given us a battle plan for how to love our wives, fellas. Not only does the Bible give us promises, but it also tells us what our uniform should be.

> *"Wherefore take unto you the whole armour of God that ye may be able to withstand in the evil day, and having done all, to stand. Stand therefore, having your loins girt about with truth, and having on the breastplate of righteousness" (Ephesians 6:13-14 KJV).*

It is all in there. Great battle plans, promises, and creeds to assist in defeating Satan. In order to win the battle that has already been won for us, we must ask for, believe in, and claim the promises our Father has already given us. Who will stand with me and declare a creed to taking His word - our weapon - for defeating Satan. We must not only read it, but also learn it, apply it, and make it a part of our DAILY lives. This is the only way that we will have victory over our enemy, the devil. He is going to attack us with his grenades of sin and bombs of depression daily. But, we must stay ready, remember, believe in our creed, and attack. Fellas, join me in grabbing your weapons, the Word. Repeat after me: "This is my rifle... Lock in down range with slow steady breaths... Aim and squeeze... Direct hit." Good to go...

HAND TO HAND COMBAT

A NIGHT WITH GOD

CHAPTER 6

Going back a little too week 3 through week 5, we were involved in learning close combat skills. We learned how to use a bayonet and we fought with pugil sticks and hand-to-hand combat. This is now referred to as Marine Corps Martial Arts Program (MCMAP). I don't know anything about MCMAP as they were just beginning this program when I left, so I'm going to go back to my day where everything ended with a good ole' heel-high stomp. We were taught how to use our hands as weapons of destruction before we picked up a rifle. When things hit the fan and you are face-to-face with the enemy, you needed to know where to hit the enemy and how to use weapons in close order combat. We were also trained how to properly use a bayonet. We needed to know how to hold the bayonet, run without tripping and falling on our own weapon, and how to attach it to our rifle and use it as an extension. Then, we had to learn how to put down all weapons and use our own bodies as a weapon. Before I went to boot camp, there were several recruits that got hurt and that caused us not to pick up the gloves and box, but we had the next best thing - pugil sticks.

I know you all remember in the movie, "American Gladiators," where these big, "swole" muscle-head dudes stood on platforms and swung to the hills to knock the other person's head off. It was something like that, but better. I remember it like it was yesterday. There was an arena where we practiced. We got in there and went at it. When we became good with the sticks, we were introduced to the real battlefield. This arena was like a maze that we had to run through from opposite ends and meet in the middle where we would have to be the first one to hit the other recruit and fight until our Drill Instructions called it off. Oh, what fun! This battle zone separated the real from the fake in front of everybody. You did not want to be the one that got knocked out.

"Mann! Hood! Y'all up next."

Sidebar... They liked calling us at the same time because this was their little joke. Get it? Mann, Hood... Manhood... Yeah, I know. It was corny to us too, but hey, what were you going to say, right?

Time to gear up. Mouthpiece in and headgear on. I slipped my hands into the grips. Let's go. Blue ready? Red ready? ATTACK! I took off through the maze and made it to the center. Both of us made it at the same time. POW! I got hit first and I hit back. We swung; breathing hard, but neither one of us could knock the other out. I got hit and rocked back. I gained my balance and swung back. Straight hit put Hood on his heels and he came back. We went hard for the entire time.

"TIME!!!"

We kept going. Both of us were determined to knock the other out.

"TIME!!!"

I felt the DI grab me as I saw another DI grab Hood. We heard the whole platoon screaming and going crazy. All the DI's were smiling and laughing.

"Oh, you all want to keep on fighting? Good to go. Do it again."

This was entertaining to them.

"Ready to go again?"

"Yes, Sir."

"Good. ATTACK!!!"

We did it again; tired and hot, but determined. I wasn't going to be the one to lose (neither was my boy, Hood). We fought three times and all three ended in a draw. After the rest of the platoon finished fighting, we sat down around the practice arena. Our DI came into the middle and started to talk. He told all of the ones who fought to a draw to stand up. All of the DI's started clapping and patting us on the back. Then, he gave us a motivational speech. My DI told us:

> "This is what the Marines is looking for - that "never giving up" attitude. If you feel like retreating... Fight. Don't give up. You understand?"

> "Yes, sir."

> "Fight when it hurts. Remember, pain is temporary; pride is forever. Never give up; never give in. Hold fast. Stand tall. Fight until you get the outcome you are looking for. Your mission is to never give up until you get what you want."

> "You understand?"

> "Yes, sir."

That made me feel good. I was proud to be a winner. Yes, I didn't win so to speak, but the cheers and standing ovation were all worth it. The four of us who ended in a draw were made guide and squad leaders. We were the cream of the crop. We were now in charge of the platoon. We got what we wanted - to be the leaders.

There is a story in the Bible of a man who stood up, fought, fought, and fought. He didn't have pugil sticks, but he wrestled all night. He was Jacob, the second son of Isaac; little brother of Esau. Daddy Isaac was old and couldn't see. Before it was his time to pass, he wanted to bless his oldest son. He called Esau in and told him to go kill something and make his favorite meal. When Esau returned, Isaac would eat and pass a blessing on to him.

While Esau went to the field, Isaac's wife called her baby boy in and told him that his pops was about to bless his brother. She went on to tell Jacob to get some goats so that she could make his father's favorite meal. He would take it in to his father and receive the blessing. Jacob was like, "Ok. Sounds good, but Esau is the first-born and he is hairy. I'm neither." Mom said, "Don't worry about all of that. Do what I told you and I'll handle the rest."

Jacob went to get some goats, returned to his mother, Rebekah, and she made a meal. She covered Jacob in animal hair so he would pass for Esau. Jacob went in and tricked his dad.

Isaac ate and pronounced a blessing on who he thought was Esau, but was really Jacob. After Jacob left, big brother Esau came in with food, ready for his blessing. Isaac told him that he had already given the blessing to his brother. Esau was HOT. Rebekah told Jacob that he had to leave and sent him to live with her brother, Laban.

When Jacob got to a well, he met Rachel. Rachel, Laban's daughter and baby sister to Leah, was fine… After showing off a little by rolling away a stone that four other guys could not move, he told her who he was and she left to tell her father. Jacob was told that he could stay and work and he could name his fee. Without thinking, Jacob told Laban that he would work for seven years for his daughter Rachel's hand in marriage. Laban was cool with that, so Jacob worked for the seven years.

After that time was up, he went to Laban like, "What's up? I did what I said I would do. It's time for me to collect." Laban called everybody together and got his daughter ready. He put Leah, NOT Rachel, into the tent. In the morning when Jacob woke up, he saw Leah. Jacob went to Laban and asked, "What's the deal? Didn't I work for seven years?" Laban told him that he had to give his first-born away, but to finish the week's celebration and he would give Rachel to him. He also told him that he would have to work another seven years. After fourteen years, Jacob finally got what he wanted - Rachel for his wife. That's never giving up for the mission, but that is not the fight I am talking about.

After all of these years and several children, Jacob went to Laban again and told him that it was time to go. He also told Laban, "Send me away with all that I have, my wives, my children, servants and cattle. As a matter fact, I'll take all of the bad flocks from you." Once again, his father-in-law played Jacob and this went on and on. This is still not the fight I am talking about. Finally, Jacob had a family meeting with his wives and told them that it was about that time. "I have worked 20-plus years for your pops, only to be played over and over again. We are leaving. Gather only the things that belong to us and we are moving. He doesn't favor me anymore, but it's all good. God favors me. God has protected me all this time."

His wives agreed and told him to do what he had to do - what God had put in him to do. They gathered all that they had, but Rachel grabbed a little more. She took some of her father's household gods and like that, they were out. When Laban found out that they had left, he went after Jacob. While going after Jacob, God spoke to Laban in a dream and told him to be careful not say a good or bad word to Jacob. When Laban caught up with Jacob, he asked Jacob why he had done this; why had he taken his family away. He didn't even have a chance to kiss them and say goodbye. "Why did you leave like that?" Laban then said, "I should and could do something really bad to you, but God told me that I'd better not."

Laban went on to ask the real question? "If you believe in the God of your fathers, why steal my gods?" Jacob answered, "Man, I was scared you would take your daughters away from me with force. Wait.....gods? What are you talking about? Whoever took them will not live." Laban searched everything. While Laban was looking through everything, Rachel took the gods, put them in a saddle and sat on them. When her dad came to her, she hit him with, "Dad I would stand and greet you, but ummm, women problems, and I am hurting." So Laban passed her up and went on searching, but couldn't find anything. Now Jacob was hot and went all the way off. In the end, Jacob and Laban made peace. Laban left and went back home.

Remember back at the beginning of the story when Jacob left his father's house because he had stolen his brother's blessing and Esau was ready to kill him? Well, this is where he was returning. Jacob was returning to his homeland where his brother had never left. They hadn't seen each other since the day he'd left twenty-something years before. He was worried that Esau would still be mad at him, wanting to kill him. So, to ease the blow, Jacob sent servants ahead with gifts. Something like a Facebook friend request. Jacob told the servants what to say when they got there. He told them to tell Esau that he was coming behind them. Then he sent a second crew out to do the same. I guess we can call this his Twitter request. That evening, he took his wives, female servants, and his children across the river. He told them to keep on going and that he would catch up. He stayed by himself that evening, all caught up in his feelings as to what he had been through and what he was about to face. A man came and they began to wrestle. They wrestled all night until the morning. When the man saw that he couldn't shake Jacob, he touched Jacob's hip and pulled it out of socket. Sounds like a good old school camel clutch from the Iron Sheik. Remember him? Jacob still would not let go. He hung in there, in pain, finding it hard to walk, and TIRED, but Jacob kept on fighting.

> *"And he said, Let me go, for the day breaketh. And he said, I will not let thee go, except thou bless me. And he said unto him, What is thy name? And he said, Jacob. And he said, Thy name shall be called no more Jacob, but Israel: for as a prince hast thou power with God and with men, and hast prevailed. And Jacob asked him, and said, Tell me, I pray thee, thy name. And he said, Wherefore is it that thou dost ask after my name? And he blessed him there. And Jacob called the name of the place Peniel: for I have seen God face to face, and my life is preserved" (Genesis 32:26-30 KJV).*

That morning Jacob, I mean Israel, walked away with a limp, but also with a blessing. He went on to meet his brother and instead of another fight, he was met with hugs and well wishes. Jacob, I mean Israel, became the father of many nations. His offspring would rule for many years. They would also be placed in slavery - hence the name "Children of Israel" - but this nation was still a nation to be reckoned with.

Jacob, as in my pugil stick training, has taught me a valuable lesson. Fight for what you want fellas, even if the odds are against you. You may have messed up by looking at pornographic material and your wife found out. Maybe you cheated on a test or taxes and have been found out. You may have done a co-worker wrong. Fight. Hold on when things look dim. The fight may feel like it's never going to be over. Stand tall and fight. When things seem like you can't win, fight.

When I was learning hand-to-hand combat we had to get in our fighting stance - strong hand back and lesser hand forward for blocking. When we threw a punch, we had to twist our bodies to get full strength out of the punch - even letting out a scream or what is known as a war cry to confuse the enemy and concentrate all energy into that punch. We as children of God also have a fighting stance. I like to call it "bended-knee". We need to start practicing that stance. 1. Down on both knees. 2. Hands up in full surrender to God. 3. Let out some screams - your war cry to concentrate all energy into that prayer that punches towards the enemy. There is no way we can win any battle against Satan alone. We have to depend on God for our strength. As a matter of fact, He has already won the fight for us. How cool is that? Pray, put God first, and fight. Fight for that marriage that looks like it's done. Keep fighting for the truth to come out when you have been falsely accused. Keep fighting when the world smacks you across the face with that pugil stick of sin, guilt, and self-pity. Keep on holding on and tell God, "I'm not letting go until You bless me!"

Good to go…

GAS, GAS, GAS!!!

PANIC ATTACK

CHAPTER 7

With so much emphasis on fighting, knowledge, and weapons training, it almost slipped my mind that I was also preparing for war. Everything that I learned in boot camp readied me for what would happen in the tragic event of war. I had to know what I was standing for in the history of the United States Marine Corps. I also had to know the right way to use weapons that were issued to me. Also, I was prepared for face-to-face combat with the enemy just in case, for some reason I was out of ammo, I knew how to get down and get it on with my hands. This was all great, but as we know, war is not like it used to be. In the past, there were rows of troops face-to-face, screaming as they ran towards each other while arrows and cannons were fired into the crowd. Now, there is fear of nuclear warfare. Dirty fighting to me. This reminds me of a boxer who hits below the belt all of the time. Just plain dirty. This is what I had to train for as well. This is where I came to know and learn about the good old gas chamber. Nuclear, Biological, and Chemical Training (NBC).

"Today, we will learn about the M40 Field Protective Mask. You understand?"

"Yes, sir."

"You will learn how to properly put this on. What it means to dawn and clear your mask. You understand?"

"Yes, sir".

"And then we're going to doggone take you into that little building and play with some gas. You understand?"

"Yes, sir."

From there the Drill Instructor barked out instructions as I sat and took it all in.

This was serious. We were going into the place that I'd had heard stories about. Marine legends were passed down and added to. They were stories of how people had passed out and how the chamber was the worst place in the world. Either way, I knew if I didn't listen, I might be the one of those stories passed down. After I sat there for what seemed liked hours, it was time to get up. This was just for practice. We had to practice putting on and taking off the mask, dawning and clearing, and screaming, "GAS, GAS, GAS!" This would be the call if I heard or smelled any type of gas. With this call, I would take out my gas mask, slip it over my head, tighten the straps for a good seal, press my air release button, and breathe in. If the filter was good and straps were in good condition, I would be able to breathe and go on with the daily routine. If not, well let's just say, not good at all.

"Let's go! Line up! Time to go in my chamber. Good to go?"

"Yes, sir."

"Squad one. GAS, GAS, GAS!"

With that, I watched squad one go into the chamber and come out. My nerves were going crazy. All I saw was smoke or gas coming off of the recruit's cammies. I saw them snorting with snot coming all out of their noses. I saw them in tears, coughing, gagging, and barely able to walk. Recruits couldn't see, so they ran into each other with their hands raised in the air. Wait a minute! What was really going on in there?

As squad one came out and some of the recruits in squad two saw what was going on, I saw recruits trying to sneak to the back of the line, hoping that they could sneak over to squad one as though they were done.

"Get back in line!"

"Yes, sir"

"Squad two. GAS, GAS, GAS!"

Ok, same thing as squad one; snot, tears, and gagging. Now, it was my turn.

"Squad three, GAS, GAS, GAS!"

I put the gas mask on, dawned and cleared, and walked into the chamber. As I walked in, I heard the Drill Instructors tell us to stay on the bulkhead, stay shoulder to shoulder and to wait on his command. I looked around and saw my whole squad standing there and, wait, why did all of the Drill Instructors have on full moc suits? Did I miss the day these were issued out? No, they only gave us our M40's, and I began to freak out. Well, too late to freak out now. I saw the NBC instructor walk to a small table in the middle of the room and pop some tablets in a little pan. Then I saw it - GAS. It started to fill the room. It became thicker and thicker until the entire room was consumed.

"Mask off! Keep your eyes closed and hold your breath!"

I took my mask off and kept my eyes closed without breathing. But, all of us didn't hold our breath. One cough was heard. Then, more coughing. Somebody wanted to see what it smelled like. Dummy… Now he couldn't breathe. With panic setting in, all you could hear was the Drill Instructor screaming through his mask.

"Freakin' good to go there, yoo-hoo. Where do you think you're going? You can't get out. Stand up! Freakin' stand up. We got one freakin' failure to follow instructions. Good to go..."

I wanted to open my eyes so badly, but no, not me. I was not the one. Right at that moment, we heard the command to put our masks back on. I couldn't wait to dawn and clear and open my eyes to see who it was and what was going on. There he was, folded up on the floor with his mask on trying to catch his breath. WOW. Ok. Now that I had seen what would happen, could we go?

"GAS, GAS, GAS!"

Again! Really! We put our masks back on and waited. Once again, we took our masks off holding our breath and eyes closed. What was this? Who was standing in front of me?

"What's your name, recruit?"

Umm sir, now you want us to choke? I start thinking about how I could answer this man without breathing. I had it! I would breathe out, but not breathe in. Holding my breath I quickly trembled out:

"Sir, this recruit's name is Recruit Mann, sir."

That took more out of me than I thought it would. I was running out of breath and starting to freak out. Right before I felt the need to take a breath, I heard something that was music to my ears.

"Dawn and clear."

Thank you God! I put my mask on; dawned and cleared, thinking that this exercise was over.

"GAS, GAS, GAS!"

Ok, now this is not funny. Then I saw the hatch open.

"As you leave, pull your masks off, keep your hands in the air, and move to the wash racks. Aye, Sir?"

"Aye, Sir"

I hit the hatch, pulled my mask off and what do you know? It was my time. Snot was pouring out of my nose. Tears were running down my face. I couldn't see anything and was running into everything around. I made it to the wash racks, washed and cleaned my gear out, blew whatever snot was left out of my nose and hocked up the rest through of my mouth. After I'd washed out my gear, and cleaned out the remaining mucus, I along with the rest of the platoon, rallied around our Drill Instructors.

"Ok, listen. Freakin' when in war, you have to follow all instructions. You understand?"

"Yes, sir."

"When someone tells you to stay close to the bulkhead that means stay on the bulkhead. There may be something in front of you that you don't see. You understand?"

"Yes, sir."

"We tell you to stay shoulder to shoulder that is what we mean. Freakin' you will be in places that are unknown and the only thing that may be keeping you alive will be the feel of your fellow Marine. You understand?"

"Yes, sir."

"When we say don't breathe that means just that. Freakin' don't breathe. You don't know what type of gas the enemy may be using. There is gas that if you breathe it in, will kill you from the inside out. You understand?"

"Yes, sir."

"Remember, always follow instructions. Good to go?"

"Yes, sir."

"Now, line up."

This lesson in following instructions in the gas chamber brings to mind a man in the Bible. A man who received specific instructions from God and found out the hard way what will happen when you don't follow instructions. Fellas, let me bring to the stage the one, the only....Jonah. Jonah's specific instructions from God were:

> *"Arise, go to Nineveh, that great city, and cry against it; for their wickedness is come up before me" (Jonah 1:2 KJV).*

When Jonah heard these instructions, he did exactly what my fellow recruit did in the gas chamber. He failed to follow those instructions. Jonah went to the nearest port and headed in the opposite direction. Instead of heading to Nineveh, Jonah started on his way to Tarshish. While on the ship, a very bad storm came up. The storm was so bad, to save themselves and hopefully their ship, the sailors began to throw cargo overboard. With all the cargo gone, they still were in danger of their ship sinking. These sailors began to pray to their gods. While all of this was going on, Pastor Jonah went down to the belly of the ship and went to sleep. The captain went to him and was like, "Really? You're really asleep? Get up and pray to a god to help steer the ship or something."

All of the sailors began feeling that it was the fault of one of them as to what they were going through in this storm. They started casting lots - playing paper, rock, scissors, if you don't mind, to find out who was responsible for the storm. When they did this, Jonah lost. Jonah had paper to their scissors. The sailors started asking him to tell them who was responsible. What kind of work did he do? Where was he from? Who were his people? Jonah replied that he was Hebrew and worshiped the Lord of the Heavens, the sea, and dry land. "Bro," they asked, "What have you done to us?"

He told them to throw him overboard and the sea would calm down. They replied, "Come on man, we can't do that. We are just going to try to work through it." They tried to work it out by manning the sails, battening down the hatches, and all of that. The harder they tried, the more the storm tossed them around. With the ship almost torn apart, the sailors started praying to God to forgive them for what they were about to do. After saying "AMEN," they grabbed Jonah and tossed him overboard. In the water, Jonah began going under and God caused a big fish to come and swallow Jonah. While he was in the fish's belly, Jonah began to pray. "Lord, I have failed you. I didn't follow instructions. And I am here now. Please forgive me." Three days after that, God caused the fish to vomit Jonah up (ewww). Once again, God spoke to Jonah and gave him His instruction.

> "Go to Nineveh and tell them what I need them to know. You understand?"

> "Yes, sir."

This time Jonah took off, went into the city, and told the people of Nineveh,

> "You've got 40 days before this city is overthrown!"

The people of the city began to repent. Even the king sat in sackcloth and dust. Then he sent a mass text out to the city.

> *"And he caused it to be proclaimed and published through Nineveh by the decree of the king and his nobles, saying, Let neither man nor beast, herd nor flock, taste anything: let them not feed, nor drink water: But let man and beast be covered with sackcloth, and cry mightily unto God: yea, let them turn everyone from his evil way, and from the violence that is in their hands. Who can tell if God will turn and repent, and turn away from his fierce anger that we perish not?" (Jonah 3:7-9 KJV)*

When God saw what was going on, he did relent and saved Nineveh from destruction. This was not the end of Jonah, but this is where I am going to end.

I was a boss at running and having panic attacks and remember a specific time when I was in a relationship that I knew was wrong. From the time I entered the relationship, there were signs pointing me away from her. I got the opportunity to move away from her and moved all the way to another state only to bring her there with me. We weren't married and we were living together. My parents came to visit the day she was on her way there and when she walked in, I saw the expression on my father's face. It was of total disbelief that I would even put myself in that type of situation. I continued to see sign after sign, but I kept on running to my own Tarshish.

I saw my life go from going well and being successful to jobless and lonely. I found myself living life awaiting what Satan had for me and pushing Christ as far out of the picture as possible. My father called me one day and told me that he had a job lined up for me in Huntsville, Alabama and all I had to do was call the employer. He told me that my life would start again as soon as I moved there. He said that he had seen what God had for me there and it was waiting for me. This conversation went in one ear and out the other as I rolled my next blunt and lay next to this woman I had no business being with.

Then one day, I couldn't take it anymore. I had lost almost 100 pounds and was stressed so bad that I could not eat or sleep. The only thing I knew how to do at this time was get down on my knees and pray. This was something I had not done in years, other than to bless my food. I told God that I wanted to leave. I needed the woman out of my life completely. He then had my dad call me and tell me again about Huntsville and how I needed to go there. The next day, I talked to some people in Dallas, Texas, (in the exact opposite direction of Huntsville), and made plans to drive whatever I could fit into my car and start over.

I started off for Dallas. I stopped at my friends' house to break up the trip and hang out with them. When I got there, I hooked up with all the fellas and fell right back into doing what we did best - partying, smoking, and drinking. We started as soon as I got there and into the night. I sat there while weed smoke was in the air, several blunts were being passed around, and drinks were being poured. I heard something.

"You know you shouldn't be here. If you keep running, your outcome will not be good."

Hearing this, I started having my very own gas chamber experience. It felt like I had taken off my gas mask and was inhaling all the gas in the room. I got up thinking that if I got something to eat, I would feel better and that was the last thing I remembered. The next thing I saw were people calling my name trying to wake me up, but I couldn't move. I had passed out and everyone thought the worst. They thought I had died right there. I came to when one of the guys snatched me up and took me outside, hoping fresh air would help. As I came too, I realized that my friend that I had stopped in to kick it with had grabbed my phone and called my parents. Not knowing what to tell them, but that I had passed out, he gave me the phone. Then I heard my dad say,

> "God is giving you another chance to do what you need to do. Get up and go in the right direction."

As soon as I'd heard that, I got up, told my friend that I was going to sit in his car, and for him to go back to the party. In his car, I sat there and thought about what I was doing and what I had done to get to this point.

> "God, if you just allow me to make it back to Tennessee, I will work on going where you have for me to go. I will move in the direction you want me to move in. Please. I promise."

I sat right there in that car by myself for three hours having a serious battle with choosing life or death. There was a serious battle of Satan versus God going on inside of me. I heard everything the devil was throwing at me. "If you keep going to Dallas, I will make sure you have that job you want, making all the money you have ever asked for. I will set you up so that you will never have to worry again. You will have every dream you've ever dreamed come true." He used the love I have for my son to try to get me to keep going. The only thing I heard God say was, "YOU WILL DIE." I went back and forth about going to Dallas or returning to Jackson, Tennessee. I weighed every pro and con I could think of and at the end of those three hours, I made up in my mind that I wanted to choose life.

The next morning when I woke up, I talked to my homeboy about my decision, but was afraid to tell him the true battle I was having. I told him I knew that if I kept going, I would die. My boy did something that I never thought he would ever do. He prayed for me. When he got up, he called my parents and told them that I was coming back that way. They thanked him for taking care of me and when he hung up the phone, he told me that it was time for me to leave. I got in my car and drove back. The moment I got into the city, something was different. I went back to work part-time. While I was at work, a district manager came into my store and told me that my name had come up to be considered for managing a store for her; she gave me an on-the-spot interview right then.

I moved away from the woman I had been with and it was right on time. She had gone home and had gotten pregnant by some other guy, but was telling me that I was the father. I found out that I was not when HE called me to tell me what was going on. I began picking my weight back up and looking healthy again.

My relationship with my parents had taken a turn for the better. Everything was looking up and I had started moving in the right direction.

As men, we have done the same thing in both stories. We have all failed to follow instructions. We know and hear God telling us to do one thing, but we blatantly do the exact opposite. This always causes us great problems. "Don't smoke." We go and light up the first thing we see. "Save yourselves for marriage. Don't have sex." We go looking for the first thing open, and I am not talking about a store. Maybe your instructions are to go and do something for the less fortunate, but you go to the mall and do something for yourself. Man, if you all have ever felt any way like my fellow recruit who just wanted to see what the gas smelled like, or like Jonah in the belly of a fish covered in seaweed, fish guts, and anything else that you can think of, know that this is not the end. There will be a call to dawn and clear. Whatever fish's stomach you are in, you will be vomited up. Yes, we serve a God of another chance.

When we get the call to put our masks back in the gas chambers of life or come out of that fish's belly of sin, God will be right there to give instructions again. The question is, will you gasp for air, head right back into trouble, and keep running away from what God is telling you to do or will you run into what God has for you. One thing that I have learned in my life, is when we put our hands into God's plan, we always mess up. God doesn't need any help being God. Men, who will stand with me today and say, "God, Your will be done. I will not put my hand in Your business again. I am ready to listen and follow Your instructions. I can't help You be who You already are. You are God all by Yourself..."

Fellas, stand with me. If God says go, we will go. No matter what it looks like. We will trust that God's plans are the only plans and He will lead us to them and give us the instructions to go through them. Good to go...

HUMP DAY

WHAT'S IN YOUR PACK?

CHAPTER 8

Hump day. No not the nickname for Wednesday that the camel made famous while walking around the office asking what day it is. That is a funny commercial, however. These days were days where we, for the most part, would walk in the woods. Some people call it a hike. Some people want to say it was more of a march, but we would come to know these walks as Humps. These humps ranged from two miles all the way to twenty-five miles. We had day and night humps. I am not talking about a casual walk in the park, taking in all the sights. No, these were brisk marches with anywhere from 50 to 75 pounds of gear on your back. We wore flight jackets and Kevlar helmets and carried our weapons. We also had to stay hydrated so that added two full canteens. We carried extra magazines with ammo and if you were the flag bearer, you would have to carry that as well. Along with all of this gear, humps had to be done in silence. You didn't speak unless you were told to.

We had to have something to put our 70 pounds in. We couldn't just carry all of this gear around in our hands. We were issued All-Purpose Lightweight Individual Carrying Equipment Packs; ALICE PACKS for short. These packs were lightweight while empty, but it was a very different story when they were fully packed. We packed an extra set of cammies, soft covers, boots, PT gear, skivvies, and socks in them. We also added powder, moleskin (for blisters), and deodorant - not for your underarms, but for chafing. Easy. I hear you. I'm not done yet. Let's add a bedroll, E tool (shovel to dig), and MRE's (Meals Ready to Eat) to last however long we were going to be out there. If you were smart, you would put everything in zip lock bags for waterproofing. These humps weren't always dry, good day marches. Some days, we would be in the rain, which added more weight onto everything that was already heavy. Ok, the ALICE PACK checklist was complete. We were ready to move out.

On humps, we took breaks to drink water and to adjust our packs. We also stopped after going through water or after a while to check our feet. One thing we learned in boot camp was to make sure, if nothing else was taken care of, to take care of our feet, especially on humps. While on breaks, we would stage our gear; take out our powder, moleskin, extra socks, and boots; and take time to rest the dogs. Here is where some recruits tried to cut corners by not packing everything. We witnessed who would probably visit the medic later.

While the majority of us sat, taking care of our feet, a select few who wanted to lighten the load and not bring boots or socks would have to complete the hump in misery. Wet, waterlogged boots would cause bad feet conditions and a heavier load to carry. On top of all of this, when the hump was over and we were all back in the squad bay, these boots had to come off and what a smell. MERCY! Now everyone else would be subject to this god-awful smell AND some would be in pain accompanied by a nasty foot fungus. Not good… You'd think that it would be recruits who got in trouble. No, squad leaders were punished. Punished for not making sure that our fellow recruits were ready. We would be the ones getting smoked for failure to follow instructions.

It only took me one time to make changes and know that even though we can scream and holler at our squad members, there still were those who were going to try to lighten the load. After that first smoke session, I started packing extra things like socks and moleskin. This way, I could at least make sure that I wouldn't have to worry about the smell with powder and these extra items. I would still get smoked, regardless.

We were taught a valuable lesson in "No Marine Left Behind" no matter what we had to do. Your pack may be lighter, but we would have to make ours heavy to ensure our fellow squad members were taken care of. "No Marine Left Behind" also meant we knew that if one of our fellow recruits had problems completing the hump, we would take on his gear to give him a break. They still had to march, but we would carry our pack AND theirs so they would not fall out. No matter what we felt like or how we felt about them, we were leaders and could not allow them to not finish. We were determined that all would finish no matter the cost we had to endure.

All this ALICE PACK talk has given me a thought. I am thinking about a man who carried the BIGGEST ALICE PACK ever. The one that no matter how much we as men try to lighten our own loads, He would always have what we needed in His pack. My big brother, Jesus. If you don't know Him, I think you need to check Him out. Jesus - Son of God, one of the three members of the Holy Trinity, mankind's guide. Jesus, a perfect being who took on humanity so that we could be saved. Born to earthly parents, Mary and Joseph, Jesus grew up as a mortal. He was faced with every sin and problem we have ever been faced with from childhood into manhood. He began His ministry at an early age. God saw that mankind, even with all the instructions of what we needed to put in our ALICE PACKS, was still trying to lighten its own load by cheating the system. This man, my big brother, took the punishment for us. He packed extra socks of salvation and moleskin of forgiveness in His pack so that we would be taken care of. Just like in the Marine Corps, no matter how much extra squad leaders did, there were always those who turned their backs on us. Jesus had the same thing happen to Him. At the last supper, Jesus turned to his twelve homeboys, the disciples, and said,

> *".... Verily I say unto you, One of you which eateth with me shall betray me. And they began to be sorrowful, and to say unto him one by one, Is it I? and another said, Is it I? And he answered and said unto them, It is one of the twelve that dippeth with me in the dish" (Mark 14:18-20 KJV).*

After this Jesus and the disciples partook of the Last Supper. They sang and Jesus talked, directing his comments to Peter in a one-on-one conversation. Peter was like, "That will not be me. I would never be the one to turn my back on You."

> *"And Jesus saith unto him, Verily I say unto thee, That this day, even in this night, before the cock crow twice, thou shalt deny me thrice" (Mark 14:30 KJV).*

Then Jesus took Peter, James, and John up to the mountain where he asked them to watch and pray. With sweat and blood pouring from Him, Jesus came back three times to check on His closest homies to see if they were praying for Him and watching out for what He knew was about to happen. Each of the three times, He found them knocked out - asleep. After the third time checking on them, He told them to get up because the hour and the enemy were coming. To make matters worse, Judas, who had a side hustle with those who wanted to kill the man that he walked with every day and learned lessons from, showed up. He came to betray Jesus with a kiss on the cheek and Jesus was arrested there.

While Jesus was before of the Sanhedrin as they tried to pin a crime on Him, Peter stood out in the courtyard where a little servant girl noticed him. She went to Peter and said,

"You also were with the Nazarene, Jesus."

"Little girl, I don't know or understand what you are talking about."

Later, she saw Peter again and she spoke up to the crowd that was around, saying he was one of them.

"Nope. Sorry. Wrong person."

As the crowd looked at him, they began saying,

"You've got to be one of them. You are Galilean."

This time Peter went all the way in and started to cuss, yell, and tell the crowd,

"I don't know this dude that you keep talking about."

In the meantime, Peter heard something in the distance. Yep, that was it; he heard the rooster crow for the third time. When he remembered what Jesus told him, he broke down and cried. As the night went on, it was decided to crucify Jesus. They mocked Him, laughed at Him, and the end result was to hang Him on a cross. He died for the sins of man. Now, that's a heavy ALICE PACK to carry; all of man's sins from the beginning of time to, well, the end. Just look at your life. What sins have you committed in just the last year? Now, multiply those sins by your age and add the sins of every man, woman, boy, and girl that has ever lived. WHOA!!! Here I am trippin about my 70-pound pack with some extra socks.

Fellas, what's in your packs? I believe it's time to take inventory of what we are supposed to have in there. Are we carrying around what is right? Or are we too busy depending on others to take our loads for us? In that pack of wrongs that we have on our backs, did we not pack forgiveness for our fellow brother? Or are we good with letting the burden of shame and guilt fall on him? How many times has someone come to you with something that you have done towards him and you turned the blame around on him, making him feel like it was his fault for how he feels instead of looking at the wrong we have done towards him? Did we remember to pack that extra love for our wives? What about instead of coming home and flopping down on the couch and watching everything on TV, you tell her to get dressed and go on a date with her for no reason, but just because. Or is she having to carry around the feeling of, "he loves me, but I just wish he knew how to love me my way?"

What if Jesus took some things out of his ALICE PACK? Where would we be? Let's not even go deep. Let's just say that if He took an extra breath out of His pack for us, would we be able to breathe on our own? Jesus filled His pack with love, forgiveness, and mercy for us to use every day. Those are not the only things that are in His pack. He has also taken our sins and shortcomings and has put them in His pack for us. Why is it so hard for us to pack forgiveness and love towards our fellow man? What are we holding onto these things for? Time to do an ALICE PACK inspection. Are we ready for the journey? Let's not wait until it is too late when we need something and it's not there. Not packing the proper materials because we want the hump to be easy is nothing but selfishness. And where selfishness is, God cannot be.

Men, pack up and ready your gear. It's HUMP DAY. Good to go...

ATTENTION

TO

DETAIL

INSPECTION

CHAPTER 9

During Marine Corps boot camp, as you have already read, I have been involved in many different things. Things such as physical training, hand-to-hand combat, classes, and humps. One thing I had the worst time understanding was that we had to be neat during all of the sweating and moving from one location to the next as well as firing on the rifle range. In my mind, as soon as I woke up, I got dirty. I had to low-crawl through dirt with the sun beating down on me and rain falling on me and through sand pits and sand fleas. Whatever I did was dirty. What sense did it make to keep things so perfectly? As in everything in boot camp, I quickly found out that this is what Marines do. We look good. To make sure we did look good, we had inspections on top of inspections on top of inspections. We had medical inspections, barracks inspections, rifle or arms inspections, and uniform inspections. Yes, the uniform that we were going to get all dirty and muddy. We had to spend hours with scissors and lighters cutting or burning off every little string that hung from our uniforms. From head to ankle, we cut off those dreaded "Irish Pennants." Even now as a civilian, I find myself not only pulling off long threads that hang, but also checking seams for the little Irish Pennants.

What is an Irish Pennant? The history and definition of this pennant comes from the Royal Navy during the time of sailing ships. It is a loose or untidy end of a line or rope (Wiktionary.org). The Marines took the name and called loose threads on a uniform Irish Pennants. It is a sure way to get your Drill Instructor in your face during inspections. Before I became a Marine, I purchased clothes and never thought twice about the little strings that were hanging off of them. Sure, I pulled the long ones off, but I had to look really hard to find the ones that no one could see besides me. Nope! Didn't care. But PM (Post Marines), I can't stand them.

Where was I? Oh yeah, boot camp. We sometimes sat on our footlockers, spending all day Sunday - the only day we had "off" - cutting and burning these IP's off of our uniforms. We still looked good in uniform with these strings hanging off of them, but they were teaching us a lesson - attention to detail. This wasn't the only thing we had to do. We spent the rest of the day making sure our boots were polished. No, let me rephrase that - making our boots look like glass.

"I wanna freakin' see my pretty reflection in them doggone boots. You understand?"

So did I. To make them look like glass, I learned tricks that were passed down from past Marines. With a rag, water, polish, and a lighter, I rubbed, polished, and buffed my boots until I didn't need the sun. I could literally put my boots up and work off of the shine. Polishing them was good, but it was the attention to detail that counted. Not only was all of this attention to detail for cammie inspections, but it was for any uniform of the day inspections as well. We had to make sure that all of the metal on our uniforms wasn't chipped or scratched. We checked the placement of our chevrons on the uniform. We even had to make sure that our belt buckles were shiny and polished. We made sure there was no rust on the buckle and even had to line it up with the seam of the pants and the line of the buttons. No bulges should be in your blouse, pants shouldn't be too long, but fit just right, and your chloroforms (dress shoes) needed to be just as shiny as the first day you bought them.

We had our rifles along with uniform inspections. This meant that these had to be cleaned as well - like new. Rifles had to be spotless as well as without dust. If a piece of the rifle was supposed to be black then it had better be black during inspection. Shoulder straps had to be tight and please don't be the one to have a loose clip on your strap which would cause your rifle to fall during inspection. At that point, a recruit would just head to the sand pit. He would be out there for a very long time.

I had to practice Shoulder Arms, Inspection Arms, and every movement with the rifle while at complete attention. During this time, my head had better not move and my eyes had better stay to the front. I had to know my rifle. And at the end of it all, that rifle had better go "click-pop".

At inspection time, we lined up in the squad bay with fresh uniforms, shiny boots, and smelling like bottles of aftershave. Rifles were jet black, straps were tight, and the rifles were flush against our legs. The guide saw the Drill Instructors walk in.

"Platoon, Ah-ten-hut!"

I snapped to attention and listened as the Guide presented the platoon to the DI's. Inspection had begun. IMMEDIATELY, they walked in front of the first recruit and sank in.

"What the freak is this there, yoo-hoo? Freakin' nasty! Just nasty!"

What in the world was going on? No matter how much I wanted to look, I didn't do anything, but kept my eyes forward and waited my turn. Here we go. All eyes were on me. Well, all the eyes that could be on me were on me. I started my inspection arms. I got my rifle snatched out of my hands while the other two drill instructors pulled at every part of my uniform. They took my cover off of my head and unbuttoned my blouse, looking for any and every Irish Pennant they could find. The more they didn't find anything, the deeper they dug. They unbuttoned my pockets and that is where they found the IPs.

"Oh, look at here, freakin' nasty pig." What happened? Your hands got tired? Your eyes stopped working? Freakin' nasty good to go, Mann. Freakin' disgusting! Look at this! What you got to say for yourself there, yoo-hoo?"

I stood in silence. What was I supposed to say, "Man, you found it in my pocket. Give me a break?" Umm no.

"Oh, you too good to answer my question, Mann? Oh no! We gone have fun. Don't button nothing up. Just stand there - the nasty, unsat recruit you are. Good to go there, Mr. Squad leader."

What in the world had just happened? Why was I standing here with my cover on inside out, turned to the side like a gangster, blouse unbuttoned, and my rifle in my arms like I was Gomer Pyle. After the inspection was done, we headed to our favorite place - the sand pits. I still didn't understand why I was getting smoked this time. Then it hit me. They had to go through all of that trouble just to find something and this was my first inspection. I must have done a good job, but what were they going to do, sit a few of us out and smoke the rest? That wouldn't be fun for them.

As boot camp went on, the inspections became easier, not because they stopped looking for things, but because we began paying attention to detail. What took hours in the beginning of boot camp only took close to thirty minutes. Not only did I buy into the fact that Marines look better than all of the other branches of service (Yeah, I'm biased. So what?), but I bought into the fact that in life there are things that we are going to see right in front of our faces, but there also will be things that we have to look closer for. Traps that are set by the devil to trip us up. These booby traps are never out in the open. Traps that may seem like nothing and look good to the human eye, but may turn out to be the exact thing that trips us up and causes us to miss out on our blessings.

Close order drill was a type of inspection as well. We were graded on tightness of formations, movement as a unit, and the rifle manual. If you were supposed to be on your left foot, it should sound like one thunderous step, not a whole bunch of individuals walking. If the platoons were nasty and couldn't get it together, they were made to stand off the parade field and watch the remaining platoons. Not trying to toot my own horn, but Platoon 3033 Kilo Company 3rd Battalion was pretty doggone good. You understand. Winners of all drill competitions, we were the business. We would get on the parade deck and other drill instructors from other battalions would bring their platoons over to watch us. From forward march to ready halt, we were the best in the business. From looking good on and off the parade deck, we stood out. These inspections taught me one thing and that was to be the best. Stand out from the crowd. Stand up and be recognized for good not because of being trash or "freakin' nasty yoo-hoos." In order to maintain this type of attitude, I had to start paying attention to detail. Sure, military regulations say that the uniform should be clean, neat, and boots dusted off. Sure, I could be just like the rest of the Marines and just not have anything to worry about, but I wanted to stand out. I wanted it to be that when I came into a room, people would look up, recognize me, and know that my standards were not just bare minimum. I can't settle for second when first is so easy to achieve. I have to pay attention to detail.

The bible talks about a time where God looked on the earth and saw his sons falling for the daughters of man. This was a time where there was so much wickedness that God made a decision.

> *"And the LORD said, I will destroy man whom I have created from the face of the earth; both man, and beast, and the creeping thing, and the fowls of the air; for it repenteth me that I have made them. But Noah found grace in the eyes of the LORD"* *(Genesis 6:7-8 KJV).*

Noah found favor. He stood out from the rest during the great inspection of the world. In Genesis 6, you can read the inspection checklist for yourself, but some of the things were:

- Righteousness ☑
- Blamelessness ☑
- Faithful walk with God ☑

Just to name a few. When God looked and saw the entire world, not just a city, but, the whole world had become full of violence and everyone else failed the inspection, He had to do something.

> *"And God said unto Noah, The end of all flesh is come before me; for the earth is filled with violence through them; and, behold, I will destroy them with the earth" (Genesis 6:13 KJV).*

God gave specific instructions as to what to do next. Attention to detail is all in these instructions.

- Build an Ark out of **cypress wood.**
- Coat it with **pitch** inside and out.

God even gave the exact measurements of the ark.

- **300 cubits** long x **50 cubits** wide x **30 cubits** high
- Put a roof on it with a **1-cubit** high opening.
- Put a **door** on it.

- Make it **three levels.**

God also told Noah who to bring along on this boat ride.

- **You**
- **Your wife**
- **Your three sons**
- **Your three sons' wives**

Then God went on to tell him how many of each animal to bring into the ark.

- **Two** of every kind and make sure they are **male and female.**

With these instructions, Noah did exactly what God told him to do. Once the ark was complete and God did a final inspection of the ark, the animals came. Noah and his family also were able to enter the ark. Here is what you may not know. There had never been rain on the earth and definitely not the amount of water that was needed to float the ark. So all of the rest of the people laughed and mocked Noah and went about life as normal. But one day something happened. Something that would change life as they knew it. It started raining. Water came from the sky as well as from under the ground. For forty days it rained. During this time, everything on the earth was destroyed. Everything and everyone except Noah, his family, and the animals on the ark.

After it stopped raining and God told him that it was OK, Noah opened the window and sent out a raven. The raven came back with nothing. Noah sent out a dove, but it came back with nothing as well. He waited another week and sent a dove back out again. When the dove came back this time, it had a fresh, new olive branch in its beak. This meant there was land. Later on, God told Noah that it was all good to come out and to bring everything out with him onto dry land. Noah built an altar to God and God was pleased. Because of Noah's attention to detail in serving God in light and in darkness, God saved Noah and his family. He also made a covenant with Noah saying:

> *"And the LORD smelled a sweet savour; and the LORD said in his heart, I will not again curse the ground any more for man's sake; for the imagination of man's heart is evil from his youth; neither will I again smite any more everything living, as I have done" (Genesis 8:21 KJV).*

God told Noah and his sons to be fruitful and replenish the earth. He also promised that he would never do send a flood again and set a rainbow in the heavens as a sign that a flood would not destroy the earth again.

Now, I didn't have the promise to hold onto in the Marines, but I believe my attention to detail was good reason why I became and stayed squad leader throughout boot camp. Now I pay close attention to every detail of my life so that God will be able to find favor with my life. What about you, fellas? Are you getting ready for that final inspection? Are you cutting off those Irish Pennants of lust, drugs, theft, and whatever else is on the uniform of your life? True, you may look good to the human eye the way you look right now, but what in your life needs some attention to detail? This is when we need to take the time to see what is not Christ-like in our characters and remove those things.

> *"Create in me a clean heart, O God; And renew a right spirit within me" (Psalms 51:10 KJV).*

When God's final inspection takes place and God comes back to get His people, what do you want your grade to be - pass or fail? I don't know about you, but I am paying attention to detail so that I can have a passing score. I know what happens when you pass and when you fail. Passing God's final inspection gets you life with Him for eternity. Failing – well, there is another place for you. It's eternal as well, but it's eternal damnation. Let's take time to get ready for that inspection. Clean off your weapon and scrub the Word. Make sure to read the instructions and understand what is being asked of you. Cut off those Irish Pennants called sin. Press your hearts out and polish your lives so that when you stand, you'll stand out from the crowd. Guys, time is getting short. I want us all to be able to stand side by side on the winning team. Platoon, let's pay attention to detail and get ready for this inspection. Good to go…

THE CRUCIBLE

SLEEP DEPRIVATION

CHAPTER 10

I had been on this island for 11 weeks at this point. I knew that time was short. We were in team week and had a little more down time. This week was time where we split the platoon into two groups. The majority of us served in the chow halls. Our platoon was assigned to the Ladies of Parris Island, the fourth battalion. I was excited to finally get to see some women. I mean, we Marines are not like the rest of the branches. We didn't train with the women, so it had been a long time since I had seen or had been around a woman, so this was very exciting for me. But wait, I did say we got split into two groups. Yeah, the other group stayed in the barracks and got their uniforms and the rest of the platoon's uniforms ready for final inspections and graduation. So, about going to the 4th battalion and checking out some ladies... Unfortunately, I was put in charge of the Barracks Marines. Oh joy. I didn't get to experience Fourth Battalion, but either way, I wasn't training and I got some well-needed rest. I had to choose between rest or women... Well, it wasn't my choice, but you get the point. I had a little more time to rest, but this couldn't be the end. This was not how my time on this island was going to end. It couldn't. No, this was just the quiet before the storm, so I was going to take as much time as I could to get as much rest as I could because week 12 was coming. Week 12 was all about the Crucible.

The Crucible was 54 hours in which only eight hours were dedicated to sleep. You also only got two MRE's each to ration out during those hours. I spent the day before we left packing as all recruits did. Getting ready for God only knows what. With my ALICE PACK fully stocked, staged, and ready to go, I lay down for a nap. At 0200 hours, I was awakened and told to get my gear and report to the parade deck. About an hour later, we were off to what we had only heard about and what we heard was nothing in comparison to what was about to happen.

We started out with a six-mile night road march out to an abandoned airfield. Here is where we would stage our gear and get right to it. Even though we weren't Marines yet, we saw our DI's take their DI smokies off and wear regular soft covers like we were wearing. They opened up and talked to us like regular humans instead of screaming and yelling. When we got out to the airfield, we went through several motivation courses. These stages were named after Marines that had paid the ultimate price. Some had fallen on grenades to save the lives of their squads in war while others are Marines who pulled squad members out of the line of fire one at a time until each member of his squad was pulled to safety. Our DI's would tell us the stories of these Marines and put together object lessons that we would take away from each event. These were called Warrior Stations. We were given a situation and we had to come up with the solution to each problem. Some would be as simple as clearing out of a simulated submerged Helo and the best way to do it. Others were more challenging like carrying a wounded Marine through several obstacles along with all gear, ammo cans, and communication equipment. As the day started, things were cool. I was going through the events with my squad, but we were working harder because everyone wanted to do it his way.

As the day wore on, we started figuring something out. We couldn't make it without each other. We had to lean on each other to make it. The Crucible was the culmination of everything we had gone through during the entire boot camp. Now, we had to do everything as a team. All of the screaming, running, attacking, O course obstacles, and rifle training all came back around. This was what we had trained for during the past two months.

Besides the challenging warrior stations, we also had to do a night march. This was no light walk up the road. No, this was a fast-paced march through the rough. Not to mention, it was at night, so visibility was at a bare minimum. We tripped over things would have been easily recognizable during the day, but since it was night, looking down was not an option. We tripped over the smallest things. Once one recruit tripped, it would set off a chain reaction of fellow recruits falling on top of each other. This made it that much harder. How could you move in stealth mode when you had everything and everybody falling on top of you?

After the night march, we were able to get our first four of eight hours of sleep. We pitched camp and were out for the count. Those four hours only felt like I had blinked, but it was four hours later and we were right back into the swing of things. In the field, we still had to shave and keep up our hygiene, so we used the first part of the morning trying to figure out how to shave with no mirror, limited water, and VERY LITTLE shaving cream. Let's just say that there were a lot of cuts, missed areas, and re-shaves, which is never a good thing especially without shaving cream... OUCH...

The second day began. This day was worse that the day before. I was working off of four hours of sleep and one MRE. We went through more warrior stations and team-building exercises. These team-building exercises were the hardest. I wasn't about team-building anymore. I was tired and so were the other recruits. We fought constantly and got on each other's nerves. At this point, my DI stopped the training about halfway into the day and pulled us together to remind us that we had come too far to allow separation to set in. This was the time that we needed to dig in and work as a team even more. To prove this point, we went to the next exercise - a mini O course. No biggie; I did this before by myself. As a matter of fact, I've done this twice by myself. I'm good. But, this time something was different.

As I walked up to the course, I saw a gurney lying there with a mannequin representing a fallen Marine on it. The object was to complete the O course, carrying a fellow Marine who was injured by shrapnel and couldn't run or walk for himself to the finish line where he could get treatment for his wounds. I got the team together and we came up with a plan as to how we were going to execute this as quickly and efficiently as possible.

"Mann, you're up."

Just me? Wait...

"Sir, how is this recruit supposed to do this without my team?"

"That's not my problem, Mann. You're up first."

I got started, mad that I had to be the one who did this. Not soon after I started, I dropped the mannequin off the gurney and tried to pick him up to use another style of carry. No matter how hard I tried, I could not do this without my team.

"Sir, this can't be done with only one person. This recruit needs the rest of his team to assist him.

"Exactly. It will take all of you to freakin' complete this mission. No matter how tired physically or mentally you are, you need each other. No matter how much you think you can do this on your own, when it gets heavy and bullets start flying over your head, you are going to need each other. No matter how pissed off you are at your team, it can only be completed with the help of all of you. You understand?"

"Yes, Sir."

"Now stop looking at me. One of my fellow Marines needs to be taken care of and he can't get any better just lying there by all of you just looking at me. GET A MOVE ON IT!"

Now that we had come to realize that no matter where we were, from the Crucible to time of war, we would always need our band of brothers. There would come a time where we would need someone to protect our backs while protecting his. We finished this station with a different feeling of accomplishment. We were brothers. We may have been different races, but we were brothers. We were closer than ever.

The worst part of the Crucible, to me, was not the physical aspects of the warrior stations, not even having only two MRE's, or the 54 hours we were out in the field. It was the fact that we had to stay up. Sleep deprivation can be simply defined as the condition of being robbed of sleep in real life or in experiment, as opposed to being able to sleep (Dictionary.com). Robbed of sleep when you can be asleep. This was how I felt. It was already hard enough getting a good night's rest and feeling refreshed to go throughout regular days of boot camp. Now, I could only get four hours of sleep a night and train during the night and day all day with limited food. Yeah, I felt robbed. This was the reason I was grouchy and argumentative. It was because I was tired.

Day two was over and we were in for the second four hours of sleep. There was no more food and even the little bottles of hot sauce in the MRE's were empty. All I had left was the hope and a prayer that this was almost over. That morning, we got up and packed up camp. Dirty, funky, full of mud, sweat, crusted tears, and every part of my body hurting, we still had to get back. Remember, we didn't take a bus out to the airfield - we marched. This meant that we had to march back.

Things looked different. I didn't remember going this way or coming out here. Well, it had been dark so I didn't have anything to go on to prove that it was different, but something felt different. I know for one thing, this march was way longer than the one going out there. We did five miles out and this had to be at least nine miles in. I was tired. I just wanted to hit the rack.

When thinking about sleep deprivation and how tired I was during the Crucible, my mind goes back to the Bible and three homeboys. Peter, the cussing fishermen and first disciple called to walk with Jesus; and James and John, biological brothers, sons of Zebedee, and some real Original Gangsters. This was Jesus's inner circle - his bodyguards. If you tried to mess with Jesus, you had to deal with these three and it was going to be trouble. These three, along with the rest of the disciples, had the opportunity to walk and be with Jesus every day for three and a half years. They had been in boot camp every day. They witnessed Him heal the sick, raise the dead, and perform all types of miracles day in and day out. They had seen so much that there was no reason for doubt. No reason why staying up would be a problem. You would think, but after the "last supper" and even after Jesus told them that one of them would deny Him, Jesus had his three closest homies to come roll with Him real quick. He knew that they were tired and had been up moving with Him all day, but it wouldn't take that long.

> *"And they came to a place which was named Gethsemane: and he saith to his disciples, Sit ye here, while I shall pray" (Mark 14:32 KJV).*

While they stayed where they were, Jesus went a little ways further to pray. He went in. He began asking His father to take this cup from Him, but that He would understand if God's will was different than His. Then He got up and went back to the disciples and they were asleep.

"Really?"

Then He called one of them by his full, government name.

"Simon Peter, Bro, you sleep? You can't stay up with me? Get up, keep a look out, and pray. Help Me... PLEASE!"

Jesus left again and went to pray. When he came back, he saw them all sleeping again. Jesus looked at them and asked them to stay up with him just an hour to watch and pray.

Now, I am not saying this is what happened, but have you ever been praying in church or at home where the prayer starts out real well. You're calling God every name you know Him as and you're overcome by all that has happened during that day. Or, you're just waking up and that sleepiness takes back over. Those words in your prayer turn into sounds of snoring. I have been there. Let's be real; your intentions were good. They were not to go back to sleep, but Satan knows that if he can distract you from talking to your daddy he has a better chance at working on you. Sorry...back to the story.

So, Jesus goes back to pray for the third time and comes back to find his homies knocked out. Again.

> *"And he cometh the third time, and saith unto them, Sleep on now, and take your rest: it is enough, the hour is come; behold, the Son of man is betrayed into the hands of sinners. Rise up, let us go; lo, he that betrayeth me is at hand" (Mark 14:41-42 KJV).*

Sleep deprivation sucks. The lack of sleep causes everything to go wrong. On that nine- mile march, my feet were killing me. My body was about to give out. At that moment, I heard someone yelling. It was my DI. He started calling cadences while the other DI walked back and forth, telling us to get loud. He wanted us to make sure we let everybody know who we were. As we marched, we hollered, chanted, and we start seeing houses. Outside of these houses, people clapped and cheered. What in the world was going on? In the distance, I saw a huge United States flag flying. I had never seen this one before. The closer we got, we started hearing music. The closer, the louder it became. Finally, I understood what it was. It was the Marine Corps Hymn playing loudly and on repeat. As we got to a parade deck, we were told to stage our gear and to change out of our flight jackets and Kevlar helmets to our soft covers. Then, we were told to form in our platoons. What was going on? It was something big because the Base CO and Sergeant Major were with the Battalion CO and Sergeant Major and several other Marines standing at attention.

Guys, sleep deprivation taught me one thing. Dig Deep. Without enough sleep, our minds began to wonder. We became more worried about problems and stopped looking at the solution. In this story of the disciples, we see that even Jesus' closest friends couldn't make it. They were recruits who went to sleep when they weren't supposed to and missed out on lessons as well. They got yelled at also. I don't want to be like the disciples that night. I want to dig in and stay up because something good is about to happen. I want those hours that God is asking for to be honored and respected.

I am reminded of a picture that I saw once before. It was of a man digging for something in the ground. I could see what was just ahead of where he was but he couldn't. The artist drew a face on this man where you could tell that he was tired. Sweat popped off of his face and he was in a shirt and tie, but the shirt was untucked and the tie swung in the wind. Under that picture, the artist showed the man walking away from the hole. If he would have kept digging, he would have run into diamonds and gold bars, but he gave up. Right when he was about to receive his gift, he gave up.

Fellas, I know there are some of you all who have been praying for a blessing day in and day out. Some of you all have been asking for the same thing for years or even feel as though things are getting worse and you are losing instead of gaining anything. Stay praying. Keep believing. Don't give up. Your blessing is about to happen. Call out to Daddy. Jesus did. In the hour He went to pray, His spirit was heavy. He even asked God to take the cup from Him. Even while tired, Jesus still said, "Not My will, but Your will be done." He didn't get the answer He wanted, but because He knew that God's way was the only way and because He was so connected with the Father that no matter what was to be the outcome, He knew that God had a plan.

We get so busy trying to fit God into our plans that we forget that He has a plan. We stay praying, "God bless me with this and bless me with that." when God already has a "this and that," which is far better than our ideas. All we have to do is dig deep and stay up. Don't go to sleep.

> "God, Daddy, I'm tired and feel as though I can't make it. This night is long and the Devil has been beating me up all day and I want to go to sleep. I can't do it without You. Please keep me steadfast and remind me that the day is almost here and something good is about to happen in the morning. Bless my soul, so that I will be prepared to receive Your blessings. In Jesus Name, AMEN."

Fellas, WAKE UP. No time for sleep. AWAKE, watch, and pray. Good to go...

EAGLE, GLOBE, & ANCHOR

WHAT I'VE BEEN WAITING FOR

CHAPTER 11

In the last chapter, I left off telling about us coming back from the Crucible where we were on the parade deck scrambling around trying to stage gear and get into platoon formation.

"3rd Battalion, attention!"

We snapped to attention.

"Present arms!"

Every Marine present snapped to a salute. The National Anthem began to play and I started to realize that the Crucible was over. At the end, we were given a command to order arms and we snapped back to attention. During this time, the Marines around us begin cheering and screaming, "HOORAH!!!" Then it became quiet. The Base Commanding Officer came up to the microphone and began to speak, reminding us of what we have been through for the last 12 weeks - from processing to classes to overcoming physical challenges. He went on to talk about going through the Crucible and dealing with lack of sleep, added frustrations, and how some of us might have wanted to give up. He reminded us of what the first Marine told us when we were on the bus at the very beginning of boot camp - how who we started with would not be here for whatever reason. However, today, we stood here and for this accomplishment, we should be proud. We made it. He went on to explain the symbolism of the Eagle, Globe and Anchor (EGA). As he finished his speech, he said something that I had been waiting for this whole time.

> *"You all have been known as recruits, but now, for the first time, and until the day you die, you will be called Marines. You all have earned the right to be called such. And as a Marine, you have earned the right to be given your EGA's."*

After that, the Drill Instructors stepped in front of their platoons facing the CO and awaited the next command.

"Instructors, about face!"

As they turned and faced the platoon, "God Bless the USA" began to play and they continued with the remaining portion of the ceremony. The DI's stepped in front of each Marine. They started with the first squad. As they moved down the row, you could hear sniffles and see guys shaking, trying to fight back tears while others were in a full shoulder-shaking weep. As we were still at attention as best we could, muddy and funky, even the sand fleas from the island were there to congratulate us. My homeboy, Hood, standing next to me whispered:

"You better not cry, Mann. You'd better not."

I gave him a quick elbow and told him to shut up and we started laughing quietly.

"Mann, open your hand!"

My Senior Drill Instructor started telling me how proud he was of me. Then, my next DI started talking and said how he was glad that he could call me a brother. Finally, my third DI stepped front of me - Drill Instructor Sergeant Ruitz. Recon Marine always had a mean mug on his face and always played jokes on us. I could not stand this dude. He stood in front of me and told me to look him in the eyes. When I did, I saw his eyes watering.

"Sir, you'd better not."

When I said that, it seemed like the whole platoon started looking at me. All eyes were on me; even those that were supposed to be locked forward.

> *"Mann, I tried to break you. I took everything from you. I took your Moto picture. I would read your mail trying to break you down. Every time I did, you rose to the challenge. I would snatch you out the rack. I was the one that kept on putting nasty recruits in your squad so you would stay on the quarterdeck getting smoked. Everyone showed his weakness, but you kept it in; you never showed nothing. You have been my toughest recruit ever. All that I have taken from you, I give back to you plus. You have my respect and if we ever meet again, I will be happy to share a fighting hole with you. We need more Marines like you."*

At the end of his speech, he wiped his face. I lost it. I thought this dude hated me, but he was just being hard on me because I wouldn't give in. He knew I could handle it, so he gave me hell. Yep, I was in a full on shoulder-rocking cry. Through my sniffles and smearing tears and mud across my face, I heard my whole squad, even Hood, joining in. We sounded like a choir sniffling in three-part harmony.

"Attention Mann! Enough of all that!"

I snapped back to attention, still doing the "little boy in trouble" sniffle. When the EGA ceremony was over, they gave us time to congratulate each other. The DI's walked around and shook our hands. I made my way over to where Sergeant Ruitz was. He was standing with some other DI's. When they saw me they all yelled, "Aye, Mann!" - This was an ongoing joke while I was there. I will let you figure it out. They continued, "Aye, Ruitz, this is the little dude that had you crying?" They all started laughing. After all of the jokes, I stood there and I spoke like I was still a recruit.

"Sir, Recruit Mann requesting permission to speak!"

He looked at me and said

"NO!"

I was confused. He just said all of those nice things and he still wanted to mess with me. That is what I was thinking to myself. I may be a little crazy, but I'm not stupid. Then one of the other DI's looked at me and said,

"You're not a recruit anymore. You are a Marine. Talk like one."

Whoa! Ok!

"Sgt. Ruitz?"

"What, Mann? What do you want?"

"Thank you."

I turned and walked away. That's all I could say. He actually made me a Marine. All I could do was go back and say thank you. I had to.

There are several stories from the bible that came to mind related to this experience. One was the healing of the ten men with leprosy - how all ten were healed and only one came back to say thank you. But, you can read that one for yourself in Luke 17:11-19. The main story that comes to my mind that talks about losing everything and staying faithful to Christ and getting everything back that was lost is my boy, Job.

Job was from Uz. Good dude, God-fearing, upright, and a blameless man. Father of ten children: seven boys and three girls. The Bible says that he was the greatest man among all of the people in the East. He knew his children were wild and after they partied all night, he would offer burnt offerings on their behalf. Dude had it all. One day, God and the angels were having a business meeting and in walked Satan. God asked Satan where was he coming from and Satan told him that he was just roaming around the earth trying to see who still loved God and who he could win to his side. God was like, "What about my boy, Job? There is nobody on earth like that dude. He is loyal and fears Me.

He shuns all evil. That's the man right there." So, Satan challenged God, telling him he bet that if God would take that hedge of protection from around Job and strike everything that he had, that he was sure that Job would curse Him. God said, "Cool. Everything he has, except his person, is under your control." Satan knew that he had a winning ticket.

One day, Job was going about his normal routine. His children were doing what they did and a servant came to him and informed him that the Sabeans had come and taken all of is oxen and donkeys. Not only did they steal all of them, they also had killed all of the servants. This servant was the only one to get away. While he was getting this word, another servant came and told him that all of his sheep and the servants tending them had been burnt up and that he was the only one that had gotten away. WHILE they were talking about that, another servant came to him and told him that the Chaldeans came and took all of his camels and killed all of those servants and he was the only one that had gotten away. Man, how much more, right? Oh wait. I'm not done. While they were talking about that issue, you guessed it, another servant came and told him that he was at the party that his children had thrown and a wind blew, collapsed the house, and killed everyone. Wow, and we talk about how bad our day is at work. After hearing all of this, Job tore his clothes and cried out to God saying:

> *"Naked came I out of my mother's womb, and naked shall I return thither: the LORD gave, and the LORD hath taken away; blessed be the name of the LORD" (Job 1:21 KJV).*

With all of that, Job still did not curse God. In the midst of his tragedy, he still gave God praise. Mercy…

Satan came back to God and God asked him what happened. Satan said that he thought for sure that Job would curse His name. Satan asked to let him have his health because that would surely get Job to curse him. God agreed, but told Satan that he could not kill him. Satan left and touched Job with the most sickening and embarrassing disease. He gave him boils from head to toe. This forced Job to move out of his mansion and sit in ashes. Then came Sista Job, his wife.

> "Really. You're still staying true to God? Just curse him and die."

> "Nope, I ain't going to be able to do it."

Job had three homeboys that got the text message and saw on TV that their boy, Job, was going through it. They came to check on him. When they arrived, they ripped their clothes, covered themselves in ashes, and sat for seven days, not saying a word. Those were some true friends right there. Then Job spoke.

Depressed and hurt, he cursed the day he was born, asking why he had not been taken. Why had he not been born dead? Eliphaz, one of Job's homies, broke his silence:

> "Bro, can I speak? Several times you have been the one giving encouraging words, but now you are the one in need. Practice what you preach, fam. I was dreaming one day and was in shook; couldn't put my finger on it until I heard a voice say...."

> > *"Shall mortal man be more just than God? Shall a man be more pure than his maker?" (Job 4:17 KJV)*

> "Bro, if I were you, I would throw myself at the mercy of God. He has been known to do the impossible, right! God wounds but he also dresses the wounds too. Yo, real talk, God's got you."

Job replied:

> "I get all that. I just want to know why me. Why not squash me like a bug? I feel terrible questioning God."

This went on for a while. All three of them listening and giving their advice and talking to Job. They were his accountability partners.

Fellas, get yourselves an accountability partner. A person or people who are Godly men first and who will be there to listen to you and also give Godly sound, good advice. They will also be the ones who won't hold back in telling you that you are wrong and will give you a good word when you need it. My accountability partner and I call and pray with each other all of the time. We also communicate on a regular basis, just to check in with each other. As men, we have a hard time opening up because we feel as if we are supposed to be "hard" and not show weakness. Let me be the first one to tell you - not showing weakness is the weakest thing you could do. Get a partner that will pray with you, not just pray for you and you be that same thing for him. An accountability partner will also check you after prayer. I call that the "AFTER AMEN MINISTRY." Go ahead. You can use it. Now back to the story.

Job and his homeboys had their men's ministry meeting and went around the circle of friends as each one chimed in with his thoughts. Job began to pray and after prayer, was still feeling bad for himself. His boys went in on him and Job tried to argue back. They talked and talked and talked, then God stepped in. When He stepped in, He ran down a list of things that only God can do. I mean, He whipped Job real good. Then Job asked:

"What, you, the Mighty One, are going to haul me into court and press charges?" (Job 40:2 MSG)

Job is speechless and in awe at how he has spoken too much. Then God went on to ask Job more questions.

> *"Do you presume to tell me what I'm doing wrong?*
> *Are you calling me a sinner so you can be a saint?*
> *Do you have an arm like my arm?*
> *Can you shout in thunder the way I can?*
> *Go ahead, show your stuff.*
> *Let's see what you're made of, what you can do.*
> *Unleash your outrage.*
> *Target the arrogant and lay them flat.*
> *Target the arrogant and bring them to their knees.*
> *Stop the wicked in their tracks—make mincemeat of them!*
> *Dig a mass grave and dump them in it—*
> *faceless corpses in an unmarked grave.*
> *I'll gladly step aside and hand things over to you—*
> *you can surely save yourself with no help from me!"*
> *(Job 40:8-14 MSG)*

God sent Job down the line of what He could do to remind him of all that He had done and blessed him with. Job began to worship God like never before. Then God looked at his friends and told them, "Thanks, but no thanks. Glad you came to check on Job, but you have all sinned." He told them to bring seven bulls and seven rams to HIS friend Job. He told them that they had to sacrifice them on their own behalves, then He wanted Job to pray for them. It was then that He would accept his prayer. They did so, and after Job prayed for his homies, God accepted the prayer. God gave Job everything back that he had lost. But that's not the best part; God doubled everything he had lost. This dude was already well off - just imagine how much he had now all because he stayed faithful to God. That is a Drill Instructor to recruit moment, if you ask me.

I was given respect back because of what I was training to become. My EGA moment is far less than this. Fellas, when the world tries to bring you down, stay faithful. We all have lost something; loss of a marriage, a job lay-off, even having been a school dropout. We feel bad about what has happened. This one thing is true: don't give up. Never curse God. He gave it to you and will give it again. Look at Job. He lost everything. His wife told him to give up. His friends talked bad about God. Everything around him seemed to be going wrong, but he prayed. He remembered God's promises. He stood on them. I know it looks dim, but just when it seems like the devil has it in for you, God will show His face.

I always look at my oldest brother. I always wonder how he can smile all of the time. I mean, he was a cop in Memphis, Tennessee. He has seen tragedy day in and day out. Later in life, he attempted to save a young lady from a burning car and couldn't. We experienced the death of our middle brother. Every step of the way, all he did was smile. He was able to preach his own brother's eulogy with a smile. I'm sure he questioned the thought of God, but never cursed Him. I have seen him prosper in what he has. Who goes from being a cop to a nurse to Chief Anesthetist to graduating in Pastoral Studies AND STILL WANTS TO GO BACK. His faith and trust in God is unwavering. That's what I am looking for. That faith where, even in death or just at the bottom, I can look up and say, "God, Your will be done" with faith the size of a mustard seed. Men, let's stop putting so much emphasis on the stress of life and give it to God. All of it. Let's be Job-like men instead of like his friends. God has it all under control and whatever you may have lost, believe that God's will shall be done. Prepare for that better job, that more loving relationship with your spouse, or that perfect GPA in school. God's got it. Good to go...

WARRIOR'S BREAKFAST

CHOW DOWN

CHAPTER 12

Yes! The Crucible was done. I earned my Eagle, Globe, and Anchor (EGA) and was officially a Marine. Now I could lie back, chill for a few days, and get ready to leave this island. Nope! Sorry, wrong way of thinking. I still had to prepare for Graduation. Most importantly, I had now to learn how to be a Marine. I had to take pictures, make sure my orders were in hand, make out a will, set up a Power of Attorney, and a whole lot more. But before all of that, I still had to put my gear up.

I had just left the EGA ceremony, still had all of my gear from the Crucible, and I needed to get it back to the barracks. Just because I was a Marine now did not mean that I could automatically throw my equipment in the back of a five-ton or Humvee and take it easy. This was just the beginning. We had completed the easy part. The hard part would be living up to the

Marine name. All fellow Marines or military personnel should have shouted just now. Lots was going on in my head; thoughts of what would be next and where I would go next. How would I be treated? Would being in the Marines be just like boot camp? Wait… Why are we stopping in front of the chow hall?

"Marines, stage your gear. Time for some good ole' chow."

Would the food as a Marine be better than what I had eaten for the last 12 weeks? Then it hit me - smells of sausage, steak, and real food.

"Marines, as in the time of war, after battles have been fought and victory has been declared, there is a thing called the warriors meal. This is to show Marines appreciation for a job well done. This is your warrior's meal. Take your time. No need to rush. Enjoy, but do not get sick. Good to go… Now dig in!"

Let me tell you this. When I walked into that chow hall, I saw pancakes, waffles, different types of meat from pig to chicken to cow. There were potatoes, fruit, and my favorite - GRITS. Before I go any further in talking about this warrior's breakfast, let me explain what chow time was like for the first 12 weeks.

Breakfast	Lunch	Dinner
Cream of wheat	Boxed Lunches	Meat
Some type of meat	Water	Bread
Bread (loaf bread)		Vegetable

PowerAde, juice, or water

The meal that stood out to me the most for dinner was when we had veal and mashed potatoes or spaghetti noodles, meat, and no sauce. Sounds like it is not that bad, right? I will give you that, but here are the bad parts. We would line up to go into the chow hall. The first recruits in line would be the small recruits. The ones that needed to gain weight, followed by the platoon squads. Next, the overweight recruits would be in line followed by the platoon squad leaders and guide. Our time started when the first recruit sat down and start eating and ended when the first recruits head popped up and start looking around. I was a squad leader, so I was at the end of the line. By the time I could get my food and sit down I usually had 3-5 mins to eat, whereas, others would have 20-25 mins to eat. This, for me, meant head down, fork in hand, and a constant movement of hand from plate to mouth. Let's just say that I threw away a lot of unfinished food. Let's not forget the times that the Drill Instructors may have been having a bad day or just wanted to "play."

"You're done! Trays up. LET'S GO!"

Before you run and report malnutrition at boot camp to your state representatives, let me clarify. We were given full opportunity to eat; we just did so in a hurry. I included juice, PowerAde, and water in the list of things we ate every day. We also could choose soda if we wanted it, but soda was not a smart choice based on the way we trained outside all day, marched everywhere we went, and ran for miles at a time. Don't forget the good ole' sand pit smoke sessions. Hydration was my best friend and soda was my enemy. I am not for passing out and having to take my core temperature - the Silver Bullet.

Mr. Silver Bullet was the thermostat that the Medic took core temperatures with. Aannndd, let's just say that you or your bottom did not want that... Yeah, water and PowerAde were good enough for me. Water was for hydration and PowerAde was to replenish electrolytes to prevent cramps. The bottom line is, chow time was not really a good time. So, when I walked into this warrior's breakfast, and had all of that food to eat, the heavens seemed to open up and the movie music started playing. I was about to tear something up. I wanted some of everything. One problem I had, however, was that boot camp was designed to train your entire body, which my stomach was part of.

My eyes were, as the old folks used to say, bigger than my stomach, but that did not stop me from loading my plate up with everything I saw. I tried to eat it all, but could only take in enough to maintain. I had so much food left on my plate that those commercials for starving children would never air. There were some Marines who went in and finished one plate and another plate. But later, they felt it and we "smelt" it. No matter if we overate or ate just enough, it felt good to sit down and enjoy a meal for a change. We were not rushed out when the first head popped up. We got a chance to talk to each other and to our Drill Instructors. I was happy and kept pulling my EGA out to look at it. But this was only the beginning of week 13. We still had things to do.

"Let's go Marines. We've got work to do."

In the third year of King Jehoiakim's reign of Judea, Babylon's king Nebuchadnezzar came and conquered the land. After this takeover, King Nebuchadnezzar called his right-hand man in and told him to get some of the Israelites of the noble and royal family to come to boot camp and learn the ways of Babylon. They had to be fit, smart, and be without physical defects. They would be taught the ways and language of Babylon. They would be fed straight from the king's table and, after their training, they would enter the king's service. In this group were Daniel, Hananiah, Mishael, and Azariah. When they arrived at boot camp, their names were changed, in the same order, to Belteshazzar, Shadrach, Meshach, and Abednego.

When it came time to eat, all of what they were not used to eating was laid out for them; all of the best food and drink. But,

Daniel requested that he not eat that. He did not want to defile his body. The Chief Official came back and told him.

> "Look, I like you and we cool, but if you do not eat, you will get sick. If you get sick, the king will have my head and I am not about that life."

So Daniel asked the Commanding Officer to put him and his homies to the test for ten days.

> "Give us veggies and water, then see what we look like against the ones that eat and drink of the king's table."

The CO agreed and for ten days, they ate a special diet. At the end of ten days, they looked way better than everyone else who had pigged out, so the CO agreed that they did not have to eat what everyone else ate.

> *"Now at the end of the day that the king had said he should bring them in, then the prince of the eunuchs brought them in before Nebuchadnezzar. And the king communed with them; and among them all was found none like Daniel, Hananiah, Mishael, and Azariah: therefore stood they before the king. And in all matters of wisdom and understanding, that the king enquired of them, he found them ten times*

better than all the magicians and astrologers that were in all his realm" (Daniel 1:18-20 KJV).

Daniel and the three Hebrew boys went on to show self-discipline in many ways.

After the king had a dream and no one could interpret it, Daniel came in and God gave him the same dream and the interpretation of it. With this interpretation, King Nebuchadnezzar built a golden statue and commanded everyone to bow down when the music started. The music started and everyone did as the king ordered. Everyone besides the three Hebrew boys. Upset to say the least, King Nebuchadnezzar threw them into the fiery furnace. Their self-discipline and respect for God allowed them to be thrown into the fire and Jesus himself came to protect them. There are several stories of the self-discipline Daniel and the Boys displayed throughout their life stories. For their undying faith and not wanting to pig out on what they knew was wrong, God blessed them.

My dudes, at my warrior's breakfast, I had a chance to eat whatever I wanted. I thought about it, but knew that I would get sick and would be no good for the rest of the day if not longer. I had to demonstrate self-discipline even though I wanted to eat everything. Just because it probably tasted good did not mean that it would be good for me. Daniel and the Boys had that same self-discipline. Because of it, they were thought of highly in a land that was not theirs.

Self-discipline is the hardest thing to have. It is easy to be good in front of everybody, but what about in the privacy of our own homes. We love to point fingers at the dope man on the corner doing his thing out in public, but what about when you are in your room or by yourself and you click on that porn site? We look good at church with our nice suits and dripping with cologne, but are we there to worship or are we fixated on that dress that just walked by? Wait, what about when we drink water and juice when company comes by, but as soon as they hit the door and we see they are out of sight, we crack bottle after bottle. Hey, turn up!

We get around all the good church folks and all we can say is "Praise the Lord!" and "AMEN!" but once the homies call and come through to watch the game, we curse and use the name of God in every way besides praise and worship. You cannot tell we just came from church.

> Self-discipline is "the ability to control one's feelings and overcome one's weaknesses; the ability to pursue what one thinks is right despite temptations to abandon it." (Dictionary.com)

We all struggle with this. We have to start dying to self-daily. Not my will, but Thy will be done. Self will want to take extra looks at

Sister So-in-So who just walked in and start thinking lustful thoughts. Dying to self looks different. Dying to self results in a "Good morning, Ma'am" and keeps it pushin'. Self wants to become frustrated and grab that person by the neck who just pissed you off because that is what you are used to doing. But, dying to self walks away, and not only walks away, but prays for that person. No matter if it is not taking that drink to not having sex with that woman; we have to start practicing self-discipline.

I am tired of not practicing self-discipline. I told you that I had the biggest problem with the opposite sex. I could see a woman coming and not even stare like a construction worker watching one walk by the construction site. I could just take a picture in my head and process it later on or remember what she smelled like and would use that as a conversation starter just to attempt to get what I wanted. I knew I should not have, but that was not good enough for me. I, knowing what is right and how to be strong, took the road most traveled, was weak, and gave in to the flesh. By wanting to begin practicing self-discipline and remembering that my walk with God was a full body, I gave it ALL to Him. I had to remember that all means just that - all. Even my thoughts were a part of all. Just like my stomach was a part of my body, I had to begin removing myself from those situations that I knew would get me caught up. I had to scroll past feeds in my Facebook time line where I normally would have stopped to post something to begin an inappropriate conversation. In some cases, I had to delete friends that I knew I did not need to have. I took a stand.

Who is ready to take that same stand? Whether I have everyone reading this book standing with me or if I stand alone, I am going to stop pigging out on what is not good for me. I am going to stand up for what is right. Like Daniel and the Boys, I am going to trust God that what He says is good is the only way. When I feel weak and am thinking about falling to temptations of the world, I am going to let God lead me. If He says "No" in front of others, by myself, I am going to do what is right. Who is with me? Good to go...

GOOD
TO
GO!!!

GRADUATION

CHAPTER 13

YES!!! The Crucible was over, training was complete, and all tests had been graded. I could officially call myself Private First Class Mann. I was a Marine. Just because I could call myself a Marine did not mean that life would become easy. Now, I had to start acting like one. Week 13 is where I started learning how to put these lessons into practical use. The good thing about week 13 was that I got to sleep in a bit longer, except on days we had PT. There was still work to do. I had to settle all of my bills. Yes, things still cost. We did not have the means to access our money during boot camp, but that did not mean that everything was free. No, they kept very good tabs and during this week where we received our debit cards, we had to settle up.

I also had to set up a Power of Attorney. If something were to happen to me during active duty, I would need someone to pay my bills or make decisions for me. There was legal paperwork so no one would fight about who would make the decisions. I was also able to get uniforms taken care of. I was able to put my rank on the sleeves and collar of my uniforms. I was able to get a good haircut since we kept scalped heads with no facial hair throughout boot camp. Now, since I was a Marine, I had the option of getting what is known as a "high and tight" or a baldhead and could keep a mustache within regulations. The high and tight cut was looked like someone put a bowl on top of your head and just went around it with clippers without a guard. It was clean on the sides with no more than an inch on the top.

I remember getting haircuts every week, starting with that first scalping during processing up until the week before the Crucible. From that cut to all of the cuts I had received, which were about once every week and were not good because I normally came out looking like I had gotten into a fight with Edward Scissorhands, this week was different. The barber took his time and it literally felt like I was back in a regular barbershop. The barber talked, asked my name, and where I was from. When I got out of the chair, he brushed me off, and I thanked God that there were no war wounds. We also got a chance to call home for the first time since that first night of processing. I was able to send and receive letters, but as far as hearing a voice other than my DI's and fellow recruits - nothing.

I had some friends that went to basic training in other branches of service and they were able to talk to people all the time over the phone. Welp, not in the United States Marine Corps. I had to wait until the last week of training to hear anybody's voice. Let me tell you. It felt so good to hear a nice, calm, loving voice. I called home and my mommy answered the phone and she gave the phone to my dad and we talked for what seemed like hours, but in actuality, it was only about 10 - 15 mins. I made sure they were coming to my graduation.

"Who's coming to graduation?"

"Your dad and I are coming and we can't wait to see you. Calvin is coming too."

"Cool. I can't wait to see you all also. Wait! Calvin is coming? Tell him not to wear his uniform because I am not saluting him."

We laughed and talked some more, and then it was time to get off the phone.

"Well, Mommy, love you all and see you all this weekend."

"Love you too, son. Bye-bye."

Great. My brother was coming. Now, before you think I did not really want him to come, I did. Let me explain to you the history as to why I did not want him to wear his uniform. Calvin Mann, the oldest of my brothers, was an officer in the United States Navy. When he found out that I was enlisting in the Marines, he joked on me saying that the Marines were the boys' department of the Navy. I came back at him letting him know that an all-girls' department needed some men around to protect them. He would also talk about how we (the Marines) were the first to fight and I would say all the Navy was good for was driving us where we needed to go because they could not fight. Good jokes between the branches and brothers.

In the military, there are huge rivalries between the branches. If you tell a Marine that you were in the Army, you would probably hear something like, "Sorry. You almost made it to the hardest branch." Or, if you saw Marines and Sailors together, you would hear them call out about the Marines being the little boys' department of the Navy. You would also hear sailors being called squids. All the branches would call the Air Force bus drivers. These jokes have been passed down through the history of the military. It was always in fun. Well, most of the time. Ok, back to talking about my brother.

During Christmas of 1998, my family got together. For those who know my brother, he was doing his normal thing - JOKING. He was joking about how in the Marine Corps hymn it literally says we are first to fight. Then I went back to the only joke I knew at that time by saying how the Navy needed us to protect them because they were little girls. Then he said:

> "It's all good. When I come to your graduation, I'm wearing my officers' uniform and you going to have to salute me."

> "Dude, I will never salute you. I ain't saluting my brother."

> "Ok. We will see."

We went on laughing and having a good time.

Back to graduation week. We were in the squad bays talking about who was coming up and I had to tell them who was coming up for me. I have to tell them that my brother was coming up and that he was an officer in the Navy. So I said something and when I did, my DI said:

> "Mann, your brother is a Squid? AHHH, HELL!!! Don't call me over to be introduced. I hate saluting Squids."

The night went on and we laughed and hit the racks. The next morning was final inspection drill and, oh, we were sharp. This was nothing but the dog and pony show for the big wigs. It came easy to us. We had done this many times during boot camp. Drill, Drill, Drill. Nothing like the sound of boots hitting the deck at the same time in step, altogether to "Ah Low Righty Left".

As the week went on, we had to practice pass and review. Pass and review was the drill formation that everyone is used to seeing on movies or TV when military marches in front of the president or dignitaries. This was our graduation practice. It was coming fast and we could not wait. During this week, we also received our civilian clothing back. Yeah, the ones we came to Parris Island in. This was funny because I put them on and they fell right back off. Nothing but my shoes fit. Pants were way too big and my shirt look like it belonged to my big brother. What was I going to do? I started to think that when I got home, I'd hit the mall and buy out the place. Then, I thought. "This was not just a summer job. This was my career." I did not have to close the stores down; not like I was going to anyway. We were paid well, but not good enough to walk in and shop like I was a big-timer. Most of the time I was going to be in my uniform or some rendition of it anyway. But, I was feeling really good because my clothes did not fit because I was a lean, mean, fighting machine. That night, my homeboy, Hood and I were flexing in the mirror when the DI came out.

"Oh y'all think y'all big now, huh?"

"Yes, Staff Sergeant."

"Good to go. Let me see what you all got. Get on my pull up bars."

Hood and I jumped on the bars and started strong. We hit 10 pull-ups and were still going. We knocked out 20, then our Staff Sergeant told us to stop. We jumped down and looked around and the rest of the platoon had jumped up.

"Oh, all y'all want some?"

"Who's next?"

One of the other members of the platoon yelled out:

"We all want some. Take us to the pit."

Why did he say that?

"Good to go. Everybody outside."

There we were - the whole platoon - in the sandpits doing pushups, digs, and mountain climbers. We threw sand, screaming, but this time, we had fun. Even the DI's were smiling. Next thing we knew, some of the other platoons that were graduating with us were in the other pits doing the same thing. Crazy….

The day before graduation is family day. This is the day when all of your family comes and you are dismissed for leave. We were in formation and leave was sounded. We streaked to our parents and loved ones. My parents came in and I noticed them looking around for me, so I walked up to them. Now, I had not seen them since Christmas and was excited to see them. I stood right in front of them and the funniest thing happened. My dad, the man that I looked just like, looked me in the face and said:

> "Sorry to bother you, but... Mann, do you know....
> BOBBY!!!"

I could not do anything but laugh. I grabbed both my parents and hugged them and we laughed and hugged some more and laughed again. I had changed so much that the parents that birthed me did not even recognize me anymore. In the hours of liberty, we walked around the base and I showed them everything. We went everywhere from my barracks to the PX and everything in between. We talked and my mommy just kept looking at me. She could not believe her eyes. As liberty ended, I hugged them and said good-bye. The next time I saw them, I would be a graduate of Marine Corps boot camp. WOW...

On Graduation Day, my sea bag was packed and life as I knew it was changed forever. I was dressed in my Charlie uniform and Platoon 3033, Kilo Company, 3rd Battalion was lined up in battalion formation. FORWARD MARCH!! I could not believe I was really in my last formation of boot camp. We marched to the parade deck and it was packed. The Parris Island band performed and they were BAD... We took our places on deck. This was it. We stood through prayer and colors and the graduation ceremony began.

While standing in formation, a bunch of cheers and names are heard being called out.

"We love you, Tommy"

"James! Woo hoo!"

Then I heard it:

"BOBBY!"

I knew that voice. That was not my dad and it was way too deep to be my mother. That voice belonged to the one and only Calvin S. Mann, Lieutenant, United States Navy. While standing at attention my eyes began to pan across the crowd. I knew that if I could spot my parents, I could see my brother. Surveying the crowd, I saw a Navy uniform. I thought, "Are you serious?" I cracked a smile as I thought about my last conversation with him where I told him, "I'll never salute you."

We went through the rest of the ceremony and got into pass and review formation. As we passed the stands, as a sign of respect not only to the Base General and Sergeant Major, but also to our loved ones, we were celebrated with cheers, screams, and applause. We got back into formation and the Base General stepped out to give a speech. He talked of how the Marine Corps was on our shoulders and how several started with us and for whatever reason did not finish with us. He ended his speech by saying, "We have given you the tools to become Marines. Now it is time for you all to be Marines. GOOD TO GO..."

We stood for the Marine Corps Hymn and at the end of the song, the Base Sergeant Major gave the order for the Drill Instructors to take charge of their platoons and dismiss us.

"PLATOON 3033, DISMISS"

"AYE, AYE, STAFF SERGEANT. HOORAH!!!"

I sprinted over to my family and friends who came to see me and we had a good time. Calvin walked up and...yes, received his salute. We laughed and talked and I introduced my family to my Drill Instructors. They had to salute him to. I got this evil look that said, "If I could put you back in training, I would just because of that." But, we all had fun and talked. I picked up my bags. No more Parris Island.

Graduation. The end. What does this mean to you? Put your own story of a man from the Bible here. I am going to quickly mention what this means to me. I could not wait to hear my DI, my brother (even though he received his salute), my mom, and especially my Dad, tell me, "Good to Go. I'm proud of you. You did it! Way to go!"

This reminds me of a man, no, sorry, *the* man. This man left His home for 33 years to live in a place where people hated

Him, to live in a place where people would, until the day He died, refuse what He was trying to give. This man went on to fight a war that would take His life. As a matter fact, He jumped on the grenade of sin to save you, me, and the next man. Yes, Jesus left His heavenly home to come to this earth so that we could be saved. He was broken, stabbed in the side, and nailed in the wrists and feet where He would be forced to hold Himself up on the cross. He was buried in a borrowed tomb for us. All of this was done while knowing that we would hear Him tell us, "Please don't smoke that blunt, snort that powder, and have sex with that person." He would also tell us not to disrespect and hit that woman, steal from your neighbor, or use His name in swearing.

He told us all of these things, knowing that we would still do them. He died so that, one day, we could understand that we had eternal life. In order for us to have eternal life, we have to make the decision to follow Him. My guys, we are all in boot camp. Look around. We are training for a battle that we cannot win on our own. Men that are right beside you will not make it. Remember, God is coming back and the dead in Christ will rise first and those who are living and believe and have accepted God as their Savior, will be caught up to meet Him in the clouds. There is another side… That side is that of Satan. Those will be the ones who will remain here and burn. Which side do you want to be on? Join me in living to see our Father. Live not just to see Him because every eye will see Him, but to live with Him in eternity.

We do not know the day of boot camp's graduation, but whatever day it is, I want to be standing in formation. In order to be standing in that formation, we have to get ready NOW. I want to hear the same thing the servants heard from their master in the parable of the talents:

> *"His lord said unto him, 'Well done, thou good and faithful servant: thou hast been faithful over a few things, I will make thee ruler over many things: enter thou into the joy of thy lord" (Matthew 25:21 KJV).*

Well done. GOOD TO GO. Men, we do not have time. Graduation is about to take place and we are going to have a big pass and review. I do not know about you, but I want to be ready to hear my Lord and Savior, my Daddy, say to me, "Well done. GOOD TO GO...."

References

Dictionary.com. Dictionary.com. Web. 20 Dec. 2015.
"Rifleman's Creed." *Rifleman's Creed.* Web. 20 Dec. 2015.
"Wiktionary." *Wiktionary.* Web. 20 Dec. 2015.
Peterson, Eugene H. *The Message: The Bible in Contemporary Language.* Colorado Springs:
     NavPress, 2002.
The Holy Bible: New International Version, Containing the Old Testament and the New
     Testament. Grand Rapids: Zondervan Bible, 1978.
The Holy Bible: King James Version. Peabody, Mass.: Hendrickson, 2004.
The Holy Bible: New King James Version. Reader's Text ed. Nashville: T. Nelson, 1990.

Made in the USA
Charleston, SC
03 March 2017